SKIMMING ETERNITY

RICHLON MERRILL

LUCIDBOOKS

SPECIAL THANKS

While many individuals provided corrections, counsel, and encouragement to me during the writing of my first novel, there are a few who stand out in their contribution to *Skimming Eternity*.

I want to first thank my wife, Dee Anne, who has been an encouragement to me throughout this entire process. In addition to her encouragement to write the novel, she read the draft and offered many suggestions and points to consider. I took them to heart. Even during the time when she was recovering from COVID-19, she took the time to read and impart much-needed insight into my manuscript.

Secondly, I cannot say enough about my brother-in-law, Walter Mills, who went well beyond simply proofreading my novel. He caught mistakes that I overlooked. He even pointed out inconsistencies within the thought process of one of my main characters. When one character, Dr. Suzanne Myers, says to another character, Ron Provost, "Good luck, Ron," my bro-in-law pointed out that Ron would never attribute circumstances in his life to luck. I needed to correct Ron's response to Dr. Myers' conveyance of luck. My sister thanked me for giving Walter something to do while recovering from shoulder surgery. I believe what Walter did went beyond merely occupying his time. Thank you, Walter, for sharing your insights.

Finally, a friend from long ago accepted my request to proofread my manuscript. He, too, found many errors. He found errors that others, including myself, completely overlooked. Frank Payne not only located those areas that needed correction but provided encouragement. I have to admit that my "need" for encouragement is very much welcome. Thank you, Frank, for your continued friendship throughout the years. As I said, many others could be added to the "thank you" list. These three I mentioned above seemed to catch the vision of *Skimming Eternity*.

TABLE OF CONTENTS

PREFACE

I am often asked, "How long did it take you to write your book?" By that question, they often refer to the point at which I first began writing the novel to the final completion of the manuscript. In the case of *Skimming Eternity*, my first novel, the answer encompasses years, if not decades, of a journey of discovery through following the One who would become the ruler of my soul. But to be fair to those who want a simple answer that does not come across in pious platitudes, the process of writing this story first began when I thought up the subject for a short story. I wrote it. My wife read it. Her first comment was, "This needs to be a novel, not a short story." I was taken aback by her suggestion. I had never written a novel. To be sure, I have written several discourses on topics including theology, evangelism apologetics, and even creation science. I have written commentaries on passages and topics in Scripture. I have taught these researched subjects to groups at my church. Only twice have I written fictional short stories. As I considered my wife's counsel, the ideas and storyline began to form in my mind. I had to ask myself the question, "Why bother writing it?" Having retired about a year ago from my 35 years as a small business owner, I had begun to devote more time to researching, developing, writing, and teaching some of the above-mentioned topics. It occurred to me that I could blend these topics into the context of a science fiction novel. While many fiction novels have been written that convey a Christian worldview, I cannot personally name any that actually convey and equip the believer for ministry. *Skimming Eternity* does just that. It is a discipleship manual disguised as a science fiction novel. Its purpose is not just to entertain those who enjoy reading science fiction but to present the very tenets of biblical truth and life application.

Therefore, I must deliver a forewarning before you read *Skimming Eternity*. To the sci-fi enthusiast, be aware that between the lines of science fiction are interwoven another message beyond that of engaging your mind with what-ifs. To my fellow followers of Christ, please be aware that you may come away a little better equipped to engage unbelievers with the gospel message of Christ. To seekers and skeptics, be advised that you might very well be convicted or, at the very least, afforded the message of God's offer of forgiveness and grace. My hope for the unbeliever is that you will complete the novel before giving up on it. The novel may very well entertain you while imparting a new perspective on life and science.

CHAPTER 1

JUNE 11, 2030
HOTEL BALCONY OVERLOOKING LAKE GENEVA NEAR THE GENEVA INTERNATIONAL CONFERENCE CENTER

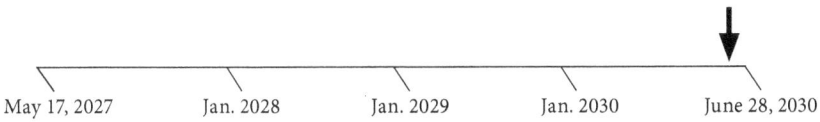

				↓
May 17, 2027	Jan. 2028	Jan. 2029	Jan. 2030	June 28, 2030

Suzanne Myers stood on the balcony of her hotel room overlooking Lake Geneva. Mont Blanc stood majestically in the distance, appearing as a massive, hallowed sentinel peering over the horizon, affording protection for the citizens below. Covering the lake were hundreds of swan sentries dutifully guarding the guests arriving at the Convention Center down below. This was the site chosen for the 2030 International Science Conference, organized by the International Science Council. Winter had passed, and now in June, the temperature was hovering in the low 20s Celsius. Many of the attendees were either researchers or instructors at esteemed institutions of higher learning. The time was about half past nine in the morning as thousands converged on the International Conference Center in Geneva, many of whom were making their way to the Amphitheater D room on the first floor. The sign on the conference room door read ISC and just below that The Astonishing and Revelatory Discovery from Neutrinos and Thought Transmission. The unusually long session title resulted

1

in the presenter's name being squeezed underneath at a diminished font size. Suzanne Myers, Ph.D. in Neuroscience was to speak on two equally significant topics. She was to first speak on the topic of Thought Transmission, which was a new term never before heard of by many of the attendees until this day. She would briefly mention elements of the study along with the introduction of team members from the Thought Transmission research in this morning's session. Her colleagues would present further findings in the late afternoon session. Her second topic would deal with a discovery concerning the effects neutrinos had on the human mind, body, and even soul. After hearing from a panel of volunteers and team members, she would present further findings on her second topic, which was near and dear to her heart.

Suzanne's phone rang. "Yes?"

"Where are you?" Her colleague Nora Bernard's question contained an element of alarm.

"I'm gathering my thoughts and taking in the view. I'll be there shortly. After all, I'm right across the street."

"I'll let the team know."

"Thanks, Nora. I'll see you shortly."

Suzanne bowed her head briefly and exhaled slowly. This was a day she and her team had anticipated over the past two and a half years. Yet she still struggled with the ethics and repercussions of it all. As with so many scientific breakthroughs in the past, this new discovery had the potential to impact the world in either a positive or negative manner. She wondered if the heart of mankind was ready for this profound new knowledge and discovery. She thought back for a brief moment to the day when she first resolved to turn her dream into reality.

CHAPTER 2

MAY 17, 2027
INCEPTION OF THOUGHT TRANSMISSION PROJECT
OFFICE OF DR. SUZANNE MYERS IN THE
NEUROSCIENCE DEPARTMENT AT KING'S
UNIVERSITY IN TORONTO

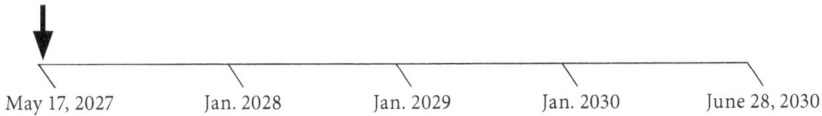

| May 17, 2027 | Jan. 2028 | Jan. 2029 | Jan. 2030 | June 28, 2030 |

D r. Suzanne Myers sat in her office at King's University in Toronto and studied the results of a recent study on brain activity as it pertained to cognitive thought. In this study, a volunteer had been asked to think of an antonym for a particular word. A video scan revealed the sections of the frontal lobe that were involved as the volunteer progressed through recalling a word and then verbally speaking it. Other brain video scan exercises revealed the process of long-term memory recall. Others had the volunteer working a crossword puzzle. What the brain scan video revealed was the interaction of the thalamus with various areas of the cortex. She watched the images, again and again, writing down the exact progression from one area of the brain to the next during the process of cognitive thought. Suzanne reflected on the many studies in which she had the privilege of participating. Most had simply analyzed brain activity. A few studies had shown how the brain of one volunteer could control the arm movement of another. "*Dog and Pony show*" was her reaction and attitude toward such exercises. She often tired of reading academic papers in various journals she referenced. Few expressed any new revelation concerning this most complex organ of the human anatomy. "*It is certainly the most marvelous entity in the known universe,*" she thought. "*Even the most sophisticated computer could not match the function of the human brain.*" This was the primary reason she had devoted her entire career to its study.

She was at a crossroads. She could continue to refine her own knowledge of this marvelous organ and pass on that knowledge to succeeding generations. *But what-if* continued to be the overriding question in her mind. "*What if thoughts could actually be transmitted from one person to another?*" was the question keeping her up at night. "*What would be the benefit?*" she wondered. An abundance of rationales gave her the justification she needed to continue her pursuit of what she called "thought transmission." Her colleagues considered such possibilities the stuff of science fiction. She reasoned that scientists from past centuries held the same attitude as these but were then shamed by new revelations and discoveries.

Her assistant, Nora Bernard, walked into Dr. Myers' office. Nora was a past student who had proven herself a valuable asset in Suzanne's laboratory studies. She was young, pretty, and brilliant. Dr. Myers had never verbalized these anxious thoughts to her dedicated assistant before. Perhaps it was time she told Nora about her dream.

"Nora, what would you think if I told you that it might be possible to transfer one person's thoughts to another person?"

"I thought that was what we do when we talk to one another."

"Well, of course, but what if we were able to tap into the thoughts of one person's mind and then transmit them to another mind?"

"Sounds kind of creepy. Wouldn't that be crossing over into taboo territory? That's the stuff of evil science-fiction schemes, isn't it? You know, the man who wants to control the world kind of thing."

"Nora, I'm serious. We could discuss the ethics of it all but just think of the benefits. Imagine this. You're a person who is trapped inside a body with no way to communicate, verbally or otherwise. Your musculature and neurological systems do not function. So not only could you not verbalize your thoughts, but your neurological system could not communicate with your muscles in order to use sign language or a keyboard or any other technological device. You had thoughts but no way to express those thoughts to another person. We both know of people who live with such hellish conditions. Wouldn't it be marvelous if they were able to convey those thoughts to another person via some sort of transmission line? Imagine how wonderful that would be."

"I suppose, but it still sounds pretty creepy to me—and unethical, too, if you ask me."

"Who's to say? We're scientists. We explore and apply scientific principles. There's nothing unethical about that."

"It also sounds like we're talking about a lot of money. If you are serious about this, have you considered the cost? I'm not so sure the university would agree to such a fantastic study."

"You're such a wet towel sometimes."

"Wet blanket."

"What?"

"The expression is 'wet blanket.'"

"It is? Oh, whatever! Actually, this isn't the first time I've considered such a study. It's been on my mind for some time now. I just haven't shared my thoughts . . . no pun intended . . . with you. But you are right. I need to give consideration to what the cost and even the probability might be for such a study. And ethics, too, I suppose. I've got more work to do. If you like, I'll keep you updated."

"Meanwhile, I stopped by to let you know that your 2:00 p.m. appointment is waiting for you in the lab."

"Oh, yes. I almost forgot. Thank you for reminding me. I'll be right there."

Suzanne realized she had much work to do before she could ever begin to pursue this dream of hers. She knew, too, that she would have to pursue this endeavor while continuing her present workload. She began to draw up her proposal as she endeavored to pursue sources of funding. *What-ifs* continued to occupy her thoughts.

CHAPTER 3

OCTOBER 18, 2027
DR. SUZANNE MYERS' OFFICE AT KING'S UNIVERSITY

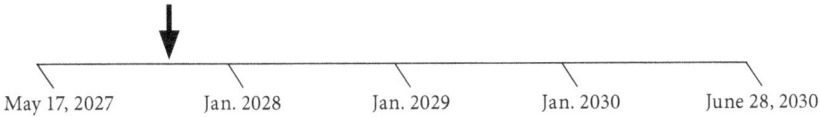

May 17, 2027	Jan. 2028	Jan. 2029	Jan. 2030	June 28, 2030

Suzanne Myers stared at the letter in her hands. The contents aroused spontaneous excitement. "They approved it," she whispered. Then more loudly she exclaimed, "They actually approved the study!" She looked around as if searching for someone she could share her excitement with. She shook the letter enthusiastically as she scurried down the hall to find Nora. She then realized that Nora had left for the day. She ran back to her office, set the letter down face up, and pulled out her phone. She called Nora's cell.

"Dr. Myers. Oh, hi. Look, I'm right in the middle of . . ."

"Nora. We've got it. The Weinberg Institute is going to fund us." Her words initiated a scream on the other end of the line.

"Oh, my God! That's wonderful." Nora inhaled to catch her breath. "So, now what?"

"We need to pull together a team. I have some names in mind. And the volunteers—how's that coming along? Have you given it any thought?"

Nora was suddenly aware that she was next up in the store checkout line. She looked back at the growing line behind her, all of who were glaring back at her. "Oh, I'm so sorry. You see . . . uh, hey, Suzanne, I'll call you back in a few minutes." She quickly ended her call and turned her attention to the checker. The excitement of this news from her mentor was mixed with anxious thoughts about where this journey would take them. *"And science too,"* she thought.

CHAPTER 4

JUNE 11, 2030
THE OPENING OF THE THOUGHT TRANSMISSION SESSION AT GENEVA SCIENCE CONFERENCE

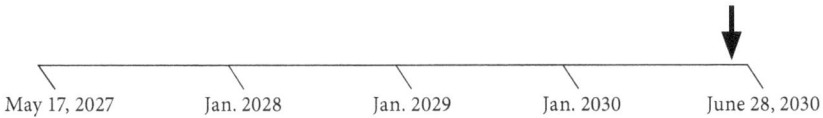

| May 17, 2027 | Jan. 2028 | Jan. 2029 | Jan. 2030 | June 28, 2030 |

An enthusiastic crowd of conference attendees was conversing among themselves. Many were impressed with the stage arrangement set before them. On the left portion of the stage was an impressive, crescent-shaped dais, behind which sat chairs for the Thought Transmission team and volunteers. Behind that were translucent panels displaying colorful arrays of light. Several large screens displayed the Thought Transmission icon and logo developed by the university's media department for the purpose of the day's event. At center stage was a single podium. To the right of it was the speaker's slide presentation monitor. The TT team was in the wings awaiting their introduction later on in the program. Dr. Suzanne Myers and Dr. Hermann Engel were closely monitoring the time. Dr. Engel turned to face Dr. Myers. "Are you ready?" She nodded.

Dr. Engel walked to the podium at center stage. As one of the organizers of this year's International Science Conference, he was to introduce Dr. Myers.

"Could I have your attention, please?" The attendees began to settle into their seats. "I can see that you are excited to hear what all the hoopla is about concerning this groundbreaking study. Suzanne Myers, Doctor of Neuroscience, who many of you know from her work with the International Science Council, will be speaking to us on Thought Transmission. Just as this newly formed term implies, she and her team have been diligently studying the possibility that thoughts from one person can actually be transmitted to another person via transmission lines. I, too, have been kept in the dark concerning their research. Where others have failed in this attempt through the years, she and her team are now claiming success. Then, as if that discovery weren't enough, she will reveal to us the findings concerning the effects of those elusive little particles known as neutrinos and how they relate to the human mind or, as Dr. Myers has added, even the human soul."

Dr. Engel quickly ran through the usual speaker credentials, highlighting Dr. Myers' noted accomplishments and her dedicated contributions over the past several years to this unconventional study of brain function.

"And now, help me give a warm hand of welcome to Dr. Suzanne Myers." Enthusiastic applause erupted as the Doctor of Neuroscience walked across the stage. She shook Dr. Engel's hand as she replaced him at the podium. Dr. Myers, as usual, preferred sneakers over heels. She was handsomely dressed in black slacks and a halter covered by a dark blue, two-button jacket, leaning a tad more casual than purely professional. She appeared at least five years younger than her 52 years. That was due in part to her practice of keeping fit, which kept the stress from her work in check. She kept her graying hair short these days, warranted by the long hours she spent in research. Although she came across as a professional deeply committed to her research, she possessed a calm assurance as one who was comfortable with herself. She was a natural leader and highly respected by her colleagues.

"Thank you all for being here today. I realize it took no small effort to put your responsibilities on hold to attend this year's conference. We hope to make it well worth your while."

She nodded, indicating to the tech team to begin the slide presentation. She took a deep breath, broadened her smile, and began her delivery.

"In mid-summer 2028, after spending countless hours researching and then months of putting our research into practice, we discovered a way to transmit brief thoughts from a subject volunteer we will designate as the transmitter to another subject we will refer to as the receiver, via transmission lines."

As Dr. Myers spoke, the audience was presented with various images conveying her words and descriptions on the screen. From time to time, one of the image displays provided an image magnification of Dr. Myers. Those in the rear of the auditorium were grateful.

She continued. "We did so by targeting distinct areas of the thalamus, frontal lobe, and cerebral cortex of the transmitter's brain to distinct areas of the receiver's brain by use of electrodes. Live digital scans of both the transmitter's and the receiver's brains were utilized to help identify the precise locations to direct the electrodes, as well as observe the patterns of thought process. After identifying and tagging these specific areas of the brain, the challenge was to determine the precise moment a thought was transmitted and to identify it as originating from the transmitting subject. In preparation for the experiment, the transmitter was given the task of forming a simple thought made up of a short phrase. The transmitter was asked to disclose his or her thought to a data collector located in the same room. The data collector wrote down the 'thought' exactly as our transmitter verbalized it. Meanwhile, the subject receiver, who was located in another room down the corridor, was also asked to concentrate on a simple thought. The receiver's own data collector wrote down that thought. When the green light was given to begin the experiment, the receiver was the first one to begin concentrating on his or her own thought. The thought was to be repeated over and over inside his or her mind. A minute or so into the experiment, the transmitter was then told to begin repeating his or her previously prepared thought. As team leader, I then gave instructions to our technician and other team members to adjust the pathways of neurotransmission in order to ensure the precise pathways were taken from transmitter to receiver. At some point, if the receiver's own repeated thought was interrupted by another thought, he or she was to raise a hand and then tell the data collector exactly what that thought entailed. In these initial experiments, we kept these thoughts to a very simple form. As I mentioned before, our transmitter was to form a thought consisting of a short phrase. I hope I have not confused you so far." Sporadic laughter came from the audience.

Dr. Myers continued. "In time we were able to pinpoint with more accuracy certain areas of the frontal lobe. Our original results were truly remarkable. Over time, the methods of collecting this data gave evidence that individual thoughts were, in fact, being transmitted from one subject to another. As our experiments expanded, these thoughts were made more complex, utilizing compound sentence structure. Eventually, daydreams from one subject were being transmitted to another with a high level of accuracy and success. We call this research Thought Transmission, which has proved to be both significant and exhilarating.

"We focused on the value and benefits of such research, especially as it pertained to those who through mental and physical limitations find it difficult or even impossible to communicate their thoughts with others. We are also aware of the significant possibility of exploitation of such technology. Due to potential misuse, our team of researchers presented our findings to the ISC, which in turn made the decision to limit access to the initial research until such time that more data would be collected, interpreted, and verified. I am fortunate to be among a team of outstanding researchers who have only recently been able to publish and speak about this study. That is why I stand before you, my esteemed colleagues, here today. Before I continue, I would like to introduce you to our fine team."

Five other team members joined Dr. Myers on stage, followed by an enthusiastic round of applause from the audience. As team members were introduced, their images appeared on the screen along with their names and title. Nora Bernard was first to speak.

CHAPTER 5

NOVEMBER 9, 2027
THE THOUGHT TRANSMISSION TEAM IS ASSEMBLED IN THE NEUROSCIENCE LAB AT KING'S UNIVERSITY

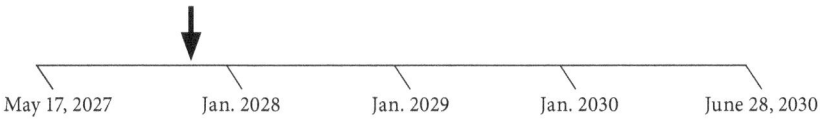

| May 17, 2027 | Jan. 2028 | Jan. 2029 | Jan. 2030 | June 28, 2030 |

Members of the research team, six in all, sat in a semi-circle inside the neuroscience laboratory at King's University in Toronto. In addition to Dr. Myers and Nora Bernard, other members included Dr. Randall Milton, another neuroscientist and trusted colleague of Dr. Myers' at the university, and Simon Loffler, an electroencephalogram operator as well as an MRI and CT expert technician who had made a name for himself in brain scan imagery. Miranda Gomez and Sharon Vogel rounded out the team. Both had been former students of neuroscience at the university. Suzanne Myers brought these two competent young women along as data collectors and analysts.

Suzanne opened up the discussion by introducing the team members to one another and explaining the role each was to take in the study. Members were given a chance to say a little something about themselves. Although Dr. Milton and Simon Loffler had already met with Dr. Myers and Nora Bernard to discuss various matters, this was the first time the entire team had assembled.

"You've all had time to read my proposal by now." All heads nodded. "And Simon and I have discussed the validity of this study."

Simon spoke up. "I've actually considered this myself. I'm really glad to be on the team."

"Right. Simon will play a vital role in all this. It's going to require a lot of patience and diligence. We hope to begin within a few weeks, but first, we must choose from the list of candidates Nora has put together. Nora?"

Nora mentioned the names from the compiled list along with the reasons each was given consideration. Some of the candidates would become transmitters of thoughts. Some would be designated receivers of thoughts. Nora had been in consult with Dr. Myers and Dr. Milton as to the criteria used in the selection process. An application form had been developed along with various tests and drills to determine an applicant's aptitude. Over the upcoming weeks, the original list of 20 candidates was reduced to six. These six would be contacted soon.

On the list was Mr. Ron Provost who had been Nora Bernard's science teacher at Freeburg High School in West York, Ontario. Ron Provost played a significant role in Nora's decision to pursue her graduate work and interest in neuroscience. She decided to contact her old alma mater to find out if her former teacher, who held a special place in her heart, was still at work influencing current students to the extent he had influenced her.

OCTOBER 1, 2027
FREEBURG HIGH SCHOOL IN WEST YORK, ONTARIO
CLASSROOM OF RON PROVOST,
HIGH SCHOOL SCIENCE TEACHER

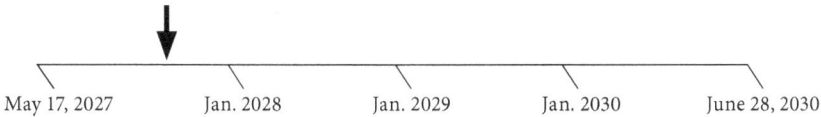

| May 17, 2027 | Jan. 2028 | Jan. 2029 | Jan. 2030 | June 28, 2030 |

Ron Provost turned away from the slide presentation on the screen to face his students.

"So you see, physics is basically at the heart of every law in the universe. It brings together matter, energy, space, and time." He looked at the wall clock. "We have a few more minutes for questions." His comment was met with silence. He was accustomed to having to wait for a response.

Liz raised her hand. "Yes, Liz?"

"Mr. Provost, I don't get why we have to keep talking about all this science stuff. I just want to be a dental assistant and get married someday and have kids and dogs and all that. I really, really don't care about physics or astronomy or chemistry and stuff like that."

Ron Provost waited for Liz to finish voicing her complaint. His facial expression never changed. Others in the classroom derided Liz for her seemingly shortsighted comment.

"Hold on, everyone. Liz brings up a good point. Let's explore what she said. First, you must realize our intent is not to turn you all into scientists. Science helps us understand the world we live in. It helps us understand the progress of discovery and how it has influenced and affected every facet of our lives. How many of you have a smartphone?"

Every hand went up.

"The technology that went into this instrument you carry with you everywhere did not come about overnight. It wasn't the result of someone's sudden invention. It is the combination of decades, if not centuries, of scientific and technological discovery."

"So again, what does that have to do with my wanting to be a dental assistant? Or George's work in Mr. Olson's garage?"

"All right, Liz. You are going to discover that much of what they teach you about becoming a dental assistant is rooted in science. First, you will have to learn the function of teeth, the muscles surrounding those teeth, oral hygiene, and probably even the structure of the human anatomy, especially as it relates to the jaw and the nervous system. Then on top of that, you will study all the instruments used in dental care, which again took years to develop. And that is what science continually accomplishes. It constantly reanalyzes data and discovery to make our lives better."

"And George's car skills?"

"Really, guys?" Ron shook his head. "Every aspect of auto mechanics has come from decades of improved technology that came as a result of the science behind converting fuel to mechanical energy, combustion, propulsion, and so on. Every mechanic is a scientist of sorts."

"Hey, George. You're a scientist!" someone blurted out. The classroom erupted in laughter.

"And class, we teach you science not just to gain more head knowledge but to help you develop good attitudes and know how to use that knowledge and skill."

Ron paused to collect his thoughts. He took a chair and swung it around, sitting with the chair's back to his chest. He leaned over and spoke methodically to his students.

"Now I have a deeper question for you. I want you to give me your opinion, not just some mindless fact you picked up along the way. Let me first set up the question. When you look at the world around you, I think you would all agree that there is order and structure in nature. Seasons come and go with precise regularity, due in large part to the angle of Earth's axis to the Sun. We are at about a 23-degree tilt from the Sun. Earth is about 92 million miles from the Sun. This distance varies as it continues its precise route around the Sun. These factors produce seasonal changes. If Earth were closer or farther away from the Sun, then all life as we know it would perish. We have an atmosphere that contains just the right amount of compounds to sustain life. This composition changes in the upper stratosphere called the ozone layer. This layer protects us from ultraviolet radiation produced by our Sun. Plants and animals work in a harmonious symbiotic relationship."

"What does symbiotic mean?" someone asked.

"It means that every living thing needs every other living thing. Plants need the carbon dioxide we breathe out. We need the oxygen the plants produce. And in some situations, this relationship is hard to accept, such as larger animals feeding on smaller ones. Think of it as the circle of life. Numerous laws of the universe keep everything in balance. So here is my question." Ron stood up and faced his class. "Give me your opinion. Do you consider all this precise order to have come about by chance?"

Johnny Myers spoke up. "Well, yeah. It took a lot of time, but yeah, I think they've proven that it could all happen by chance."

"Who is 'they,' Johnny?"

"Well, you know . . . the experts." Some in the class voiced their agreement.

"Do you see what just happened?" Ron asked. "I asked you to give me your opinion, but instead of giving much consideration to the scenario and data I set forth, you repeated something you heard from who knows where. It might surprise you that many renowned scientists disagree with your stated assumptions."

"Mr. Provost, I disagree with Johnny," Sarah Grayson spoke up. "My parents took me to that museum in Kentucky where they say that it is a Creator who designed everything."

"So, explain to me why that is *your* opinion, Sarah." Ron's intent was to stir up discussion.

"I don't know why. It just makes sense to me," added Sarah.

"Well, okay, Sarah. You said it just makes sense to you. You were using your mind to try to make sense of the things you were told and seen. I'm guessing you didn't just accept it at face value. Here is what I am trying to get you all to see." Ron paced slowly from side to side and then once again stopped and looked intently at the students. "The scientific method and thought should always begin with careful consideration of the evidence. We are in an ever-changing environment where each scientific assumption continues to undergo scrutiny. We all need to examine the evidence carefully and never simply repeat what 'they' say. Each of us examines life from a preconceived bias. If we are told that Earth is billions of years old, then we must ask this: What is the starting point on which they base their conclusions? Are their conclusions based solely on the evidence or from some preconceived notion about the universe?"

Jenny Addison interrupted. "You've lost me, Mr. Provost." Many in the class echoed her sentiment.

"Okay. For instance, if someone does not believe in a Creator who may have designed our universe but instead comes from the standpoint that every explanation for the existence of the universe must come from inside that universe, not from beyond it, then they will simply ignore the evidence that contradicts that stance. They may be convinced that everything came from nothing, strictly from a naturalistic point of view. In other words, they assume there could not possibly be any cause that came from outside of time and space. From that standpoint, they launch their conclusions about the origins of the universe and life on Earth."

Several students nodded in agreement.

"So again, students, let's begin to observe life around us and give careful consideration to the evidence before drawing conclusions. Go deep into your mind and studies. Do not merely skim the surface of the reasons for your very existence here on Earth. Do not take my word for it. Do not take the so-called experts' word for it. Look into it yourself. Read, and examine. Seek truth where it is found. That is why we teach you scientific discovery." Ron Provost looked up at the clock on the wall.

"Everyone, read chapter six in your textbook. I'll see you all back here on Monday. You all have a great weekend." With that, the bell rang. As the students filed out of the classroom, Ron Provost bowed his head. *"Thank you, Lord, for this privilege."* Ron felt an enormous sense of satisfaction in his role. It was more than a job. For him, it was a God-given ministry.

≈≈≈≈≈

Clara Wagner, a history teacher at Freeburg High School in West York, heard about Ron Provost's stance on creationism. Clara held to a strictly naturalistic worldview. Clara was an evolutionist. She felt there was no room in scientific study for the supernatural, especially as it related to the "myths" found in biblical literature. She recognized that Ron had never crossed the boundaries set in place by the West York School Board by utilizing his religion to teach science. Ron challenged his students to examine evidence and let that be the platform for each student's perspective on the matter concerning the origin of life. Although Clara taught history, she was a learned student of the physical sciences, having taught evolutionary science at one point in her teaching career. It occurred to Clara that a debate between the "proven" science of evolution and creationism would be a perfect platform for persuading students to abandon any notion that creationism was viable science but rather belonged in the category of science fiction.

CHAPTER 7

OCTOBER 4, 2027
FREEBURG HIGH SCHOOL TEACHERS' LOUNGE

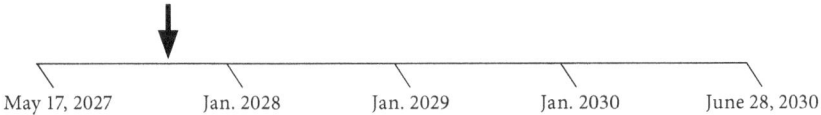

May 17, 2027	Jan. 2028	Jan. 2029	Jan. 2030	June 28, 2030

The following Monday, Clara Wagner waited for the right moment to approach Ron Provost in the teachers' lounge.

"Good morning, Ron. How are Mona and the kids?"

"Oh, well, everyone is fine. Nice of you to . . ."

"Say, Ron, I was wondering."

"About?"

"Well, uh, I know you take a creationism view of things . . ."

"Things?"

"Well, I mean for the origin of life and all."

"Well, for life on Earth. All of creation, too, yes."

"Soooo . . . I was kind of wondering how you would feel about having a debate on the origins and progression of life on Earth. I would take the accepted scientific view and . . ."

"So you're inferring that creation science is not real science?"

"Um, well, I mean that science—in general, mind you—holds to an evolutionary view of these things. But anyway, I thought maybe, with Principal Saunders and the school board's permission, mind you, we could have a debate on the topic of the origins of life and, you know, the progression of life throughout the ages."

"And where would this take place? Who would watch this debate?"

"I thought maybe we could open it up to the entire school system. You know, invite parents. Maybe even publicize it for the entire community. What do you say?"

Ron looked at Clara for a moment and then responded. "Sounds interesting. Let me think about it. I'll get back to you by the end of the week. Okay?"

"Sure, sure. Meanwhile, I'll run it by Saunders. See what he says. All right with you?"

"I don't see why not."

"Real fine then, Ron. Say, I just remembered. I need to check my box. Really good talking to you, Ron. And, oh, hey Ron, Jeremy is a fine young man. Good student. He's in my junior history class you know."

"Well, thank you, Clara. We're very proud of . . ."

"Okay. Well, bye."

Clara quickly headed out the door, leaving Ron a bit puzzled by this sudden proposition. While Ron welcomed an opportunity to bring forth the evidence for creation science, he knew Clara had ulterior motives. He doubted her sincerity in providing an honest forum for open debate. He knew he needed some time to assess the matter.

CHAPTER 8

MONDAY, OCTOBER 4, 2027
HOME OF RON AND MONA PROVOST
TORONTO, ONTARIO

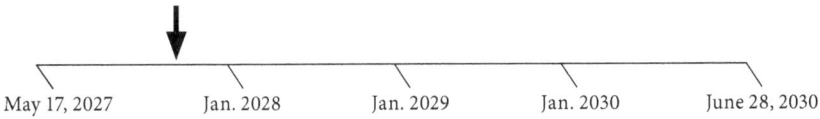

↓

May 17, 2027	Jan. 2028	Jan. 2029	Jan. 2030	June 28, 2030

Mona Provost was worn out from this typical Monday's workload. It had been a long day at West York Employment and Social Services where she worked. Her recent client was a challenge, and Mona was not looking forward to sorting through all the baggage this woman brought to the table. Regardless, Mona mentally hung the stress of her workday on the tree limb beside the front porch as she walked through the door.

"I'm home." She expected to at least be greeted by Sheldon, their beagle, if not one or two children. She poured herself a glass of tea and then collapsed on the sofa. Despite her effort to free her mind of the day's problems, her thoughts took her back to the client interview. This client, a woman, is plagued by anxiety. Panic attacks are her constant companion. She worries about her finances. She worries about her health and even continued wearing a mask in public since the pandemic in 2020—now some seven years later. Her divorce six years ago still plagues her mind. She has a fear of flying, of storms, of being robbed.

23

The woman is convinced she will be the victim of an earthquake. She is unable to hold down a job for any length of time due to her constant anxiety, which caused her to miss work and perform poorly on the job. Counselors tried to reassure the woman that her anxiety is unfounded. They showed her statistics concerning the unlikelihood of earthquakes in the area. She was shown the safety record of airlines. They suggested she enroll in a class on personal finances. They suggested she take a vacation or become involved in community service. Medication only provided momentary relief.

Mona knew from her training as a biblical counselor that the root cause of this woman's worries and fears came from a heart issue. What other counselors saw as a cause of the woman's anxiety Mona saw as the occasion for it. This single woman in her mid-30s ascribes ultimate power to these fears that end up producing anxiety. *"If only she could see that God is the source of ultimate power to overcome the challenges of life,"* Mona had thought. This client also ascribes ultimate value to her perceived need for a perfectly ordered and secure life. Only then can she relax and be at peace. Mona voiced a short prayer for the woman. "Father, show her that You alone are the source of value and worth. Please open her eyes to receive Your love and peace." Mona had prayed this same prayer for many of her clients. The scope of her work in social services was limited to providing employment services and directing her clients to other resources within the system. In her heart, however, Mona was convinced of the truth in this passage of Scripture: *"His divine power has granted to us everything pertaining to life and godliness, through the true knowledge of Him who called us by His own glory and excellence"* (2 Pet. 1:3). *"The Bible has the answers,"* she thought. She could counsel her clients for only brief periods of time. Mona tried to provide comfort and support when the opportunity arose. In her heart of hearts, she knew what these souls really needed was the new life Christ had made available to those who would receive Him as Lord and Savior.

Sheldon came through the pet door, tail wagging as he eagerly jumped up to greet his two-legged companion.

"Where is everyone, Sheldon?" Upon hearing his name, Sheldon responded with a fusion of bark and howl as his tail wagged with even more vigor.

"You're such a good boy." Mona scratched behind Sheldon's dishtowel ears. The cares of the day disappeared as she looked into the eyes of this four-legged family companion.

The front door flew open as Jeremy, Brenda, and Trevor filed through, heading for the refrigerator. Sheldon must have sensed greater prospects as he followed in close pursuit.

"Don't I even get a hello?"

Brenda, their 12-year-old, stuck her head around the corner. "Oh, hi, Mom." The other two echoed similar sentiments from the kitchen.

She heard the door to the backyard open and close. Ron sauntered through the living room on his way to the kitchen as he mentioned, "Hi, Hon. I fixed that broken sprinkler head."

"In your good slacks?" No response. He usually ignored her admonitions.

After sufficient silence, he inquired from the kitchen, "How was your day?"

"Challenging."

"What was that?"

"Oh, nothing. Hey, kids. Don't ruin your appetite. I'll start dinner around five."

Mona's words appeared to fall on deaf ears as all three kids strolled through with bags of chips and drinks. Ron was somewhat less culpable, holding a single graham cracker and a drink.

"Hey, Jeremy," Ron spoke before taking a second bite of his cracker. "Clara Wagner paid you a compliment today, saying you were a good student. She also said you were, quote, 'A fine young man.'"

"Cool." Jeremy picked up the TV remote and began surfing through channels.

Mona turned to her husband. "What brought that on? Doesn't really sound like the Clara you've described to me."

"She was buttering me up."

"For what?"

"She wants to debate me on the topic of evolution versus creation science—or creationism, as she put it. She doesn't want to admit that the creationist view is science."

Mona sat up, giving her husband a surprised look. "Really? You told me she holds to a strictly evolutionary worldview. Why would she want to give creation science a voice?"

"She thinks she'll be able to demonstrate the superiority of evolution over any notion of a Creator."

"So are you going to do it?"

"I'm thinking about it." Ron turned his attention toward his oldest son, Jeremy. "Hey, son, why are you surfing the tube? You know the rules. No TV until after your homework is done."

"No homework, Dad."

"There's always homework. And you two—same thing applies. And stop snacking. You heard your mother."

"Look who's talking." Trevor, their 14-year-old, immediately recognized his ill-suited retort. Ron gave him the look. He then turned his attention to the other two. "Now!" All three reluctantly picked up their books amidst groans and mutterings and headed to their rooms. "I'll be checking up on you later."

"And dinner will be ready by 5:30," shouted Mona who then turned her attention back to Ron.

"You're thinking about it? Tell me more."

Ron gave her the rundown on how Clara had suggested opening the debate up to the entire community and was already speaking to Principal Saunders.

"Do you think the school board is going to go for it?" Mona was well aware of the restrictions the West York ISD had concerning any reference to potential religious instruction.

"I don't know. Let's face it. Creation science presupposes a Creator. I won't go into this debate without a full arsenal. I may not be able to quote Scripture, but I need to be able to demonstrate the truth of Scripture. I need to be able to show where the evidence leads. I can't just skim the surface of God's authority and domain. Like I said, I'm thinking about it. I told Clara I would let her know before this weekend."

"Have you prayed about it?" Mona always had a way of steering her husband back to the Lord's guidance.

"Actually, no, I haven't yet. How about we do that right now?"

"Let's do."

Ron sat next to his wife as they held hands and brought the matter before the throne of God.

CHAPTER 9

THE FOLLOWING FRIDAY, OCTOBER 8, 2027 CLARA WAGNER'S CLASSROOM AT FREEBURG HIGH SCHOOL

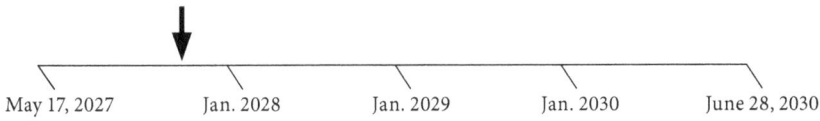

May 17, 2027	Jan. 2028	Jan. 2029	Jan. 2030	June 28, 2030

Ron Provost walked into Clara Wagner's classroom after she finished up her last class.

"Hello, Ron. I'll bet I know why you're here. I kind of thought I would hear from you before now. So the answer is yes?"

"Not exactly." Clara gave him a look of disappointment. "I've thought about it a lot. My wife, Mona, and I also prayed about it. So here's what I'm suggesting. Let's not make this a big deal—not in front of parents and the community anyway, and not so much using a formal debate format. What I am agreeable to is presenting both sides of the issue to the senior class members. If not in a classroom setting, then perhaps we could bring them together in the auditorium. Perhaps former students could also attend. Again, it won't be a debate so much as just giving the kids the position and evidence from both sides of the issue. And I don't really want to include the lower-class students. I have my reasons. But anyway, that's what I'm proposing."

"Well, Ron, um, are you afraid of standing up for your beliefs? I mean, are you not really sure of the creationist viewpoint?"

"That's not it at all. Fear has nothing to do with my decision. And I stand firmly behind creation science. And by the way, I prefer to use the term creation science rather than intelligent design or creationism. But I don't mind being referred to as a creationist. Anyway, I believe creation science is the viable explanation for the origins and progression of life on Earth. I will tell you the reasons for my decision if you really want to know."

"Sure. Why not?"

"First, I have to tell you that I don't trust my own ability to make good choices and decisions. That's why I pray about things."

"So you pray about what clothes to wear and . . ."

"Oh, no no no. God, of course, has given us the freedom to make choices on our own. But I know I need His wisdom and guidance, especially for some of the bigger decisions."

"Like this one."

"Yes. Are you sure you want me to go on?"

"Well, Ron, now you've got my curiosity up."

"Okay. Second is the fact that I have no doubt whatsoever that God created everything in the universe without the use of macroevolution. I didn't come to this conclusion by searching for proof. He made his presence known by everything I see around me; in other words, His creation. I see the evidence within creation. So you see, creation denotes a Creator. That's God. With me so far?"

"I suppose. But Ron, it's been proved that evolution is true."

"I'll get to that. But for now, I'll just say that many evolutionists have turned a blind eye to the evidence for this Creator God. Since they deny the supernatural, they must then come up with another explanation for how everything came to be, including life on Earth. Evolution, in the opinion of some scientists, is the only viable explanation. Then, of course, they not only deny God as the ultimate authority but also exclude any mention of Him in the classroom or museums, or the halls of scientific study and research. While we creationists believe and trust that God is the One who created the universe, we have the evidence to support that view. It's overwhelming. And more and more scientists and researchers are beginning to see this. Others turn a deaf ear and a blind eye because they do not want to admit that it has any merit."

"Well, that's all very interesting, but you still haven't answered me as to why you do not want to have an open debate."

"It has to do with pride and humility."

"What do you mean?"

"You see, the pride in me wants to show how intelligent and wise I am by winning this debate against evolutionary theory. Pride wants me to come out on top. Humility, on the other hand, isn't interested in exalting self or even showing the supremacy of creation science over evolution. Humility prefers to exalt God. And unfortunately, I realize that while the evidence supports a Creator, I would not be given full rein."

"To do what?"

"To bring Him glory. This debate would merely be a test of wills and skills."

"And science, remember? Look, Ron. You've talked a lot about God. So where's the science in all this creation science?"

"Science supports creation. However, much of my presentation will show the flawed science of Darwinian evolutionary theory and point out that it is actually a theory, not a fact, as the proponents of evolution want us to believe."

"So why are you in favor of showing both sides of this issue to the seniors?"

"They should be allowed to decide for themselves which evidence best supports honest scientific discovery and exploration. I cannot pretend that evolution's voice isn't a loud one demanding supremacy in the classroom. They need to hear both sides, not just the position of a school board or antiquated textbooks decided on by some bureaucrat. I'm not interested in winning a debate. I am interested in educating students and encouraging them to pursue truth."

Ron paused and nodded, satisfied that he had stated his position clearly.

Clara turned away and rolled her eyes. She reached over to turn off the image display. She turned slowly to face Ron. "I see. Well, I think I see. I wasn't expecting this. But okay, we'll set this up the way you want. I already spoke to Principal Saunders. He has given his approval under certain stipulations."

"It will be interesting to hear from him what those stipulations entail. But okay, how about this. I'll write up a proposal along with a plan and intentions, and come up with a timetable. I'll bring it to you to add any other points of clarification. We'll both sign it and then hand it over to Saunders for his approval or changes. Sound good?"

"Sure. Let's go with that."

"Great. I'll get started on it right away and keep you updated. I suppose I should let you get back to closing down the room."

Ron turned to exit. He paused when Clara added, "Hey, Ron." She hesitated briefly. "I want you to know that I respect your position even though I don't really agree totally with your reasoning. And I appreciate your candor. You've given me some things to think about."

"Thanks, Clara. Respect and consideration and honesty need to rule the day, I believe."

"Yes. I suppose they do. I look forward to the updates. Have a good weekend."

"You too." Ron turned once more to leave. Once in the hallway, he smiled, hoping that in some small way he had brought glory to His Father in heaven.

CHAPTER 10

EVENING OF THE DEBATE
FRIDAY, NOVEMBER 19, 2027
FREEBURG HIGH SCHOOL AUDITORIUM

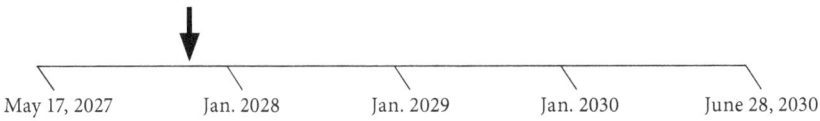

| May 17, 2027 | Jan. 2028 | Jan. 2029 | Jan. 2030 | June 28, 2030 |

Freeburg High School's principal, Richard Saunders, had read through the proposed debate format Ron Provost and Clara Wagner provided him. Although Clara and Ron had made compromises and agreed on the plan and objective of the presentations, Principal Saunders changed a major component of the agreement. While he supported the proposed debate, concurring that there should be no winners or losers or decisions made on the outcome of the presentations, he did open up the attendees to include all class levels, teachers, and parents, as well as former students. While no public announcement was made for the event, he sent an invitation to every student's household. He also sent notices of the event to alumni's known addresses.

It was agreed that there would be no use of slide presentations or images since images from various sources were often biased and altered in favor of a particular viewpoint, thus tainting the main focus, which was to solely present the evidence and arguments.

Thunderous applause welcomed Clara Wagner and Ron Provost as they walked out on stage of the Freeburg High School auditorium in West York, Ontario, this late Friday afternoon. The gymnasium was set up for an overflow crowd complete with a live feed of the auditorium stage. It, too, was filled to capacity.

Two microphones were set up on stage. One was located center stage to be used by the two presenters. Another was stage right to be used by Principal Saunders and two members of the current senior class.

Principal Saunders approached the microphone. He was dressed in business attire, which was a shift from his usual preferred casual wear.

"Testing, testing. Can everyone hear me?" He heard no complaint. "I want to welcome you all to this momentous event. We are honored that you have decided to join us here tonight. I am not at all shocked that so many are interested in the subject matter to be presented." He stood a little more erect as he continued. "Several weeks ago, Ron Provost, who is both a coach and a science teacher, along with Clara Wagner, who is a teacher of history and civics, discussed a proposed debate between evolution and creation science. Ms. Wagner will present the argument for evolution, while Mr. Provost will present a case for creation science. As you all know, this is a hot topic that generates much controversy and passion. Here in Ontario, we teach evolution, but we also teach that other theories discount evolution. Now today, in 2027, we here in West York schools believe that a forum as you have before you today can be used to present opposing views on evolution. This forum has its critics and strong opponents. We, however, are against censoring any other 'scientific' view. I use the term *scientific* because it is not our intent to simply allow a view that primarily supports a known religious viewpoint. Mr. Provost has presented his intended outline to me and the school board, as has Ms. Wagner. With much trepidation, we have allowed them both to proceed under certain stipulations."

Richard Saunders cleared his throat. He was well aware of the dubious nature of this event. He had begun to question his decision to allow such a debate, but as an educator, he knew that truth needed to stand firmly on its own merit. Evidence challenging even the most well-established position needed a voice. Besides, this event would not decide whether the West York school board would change its current educational strategy. There would be no winners or losers as is usually the intent of a debate. Both sides were given the opportunity to support their positions. He strained to see faces in the audience in an attempt to get a feel for the audience. He could not.

"Now let me point out that this is not a debate in the truest sense of the word. Debates are usually meant to help decide a position on any given controversial subject. You are probably familiar with political debates where each candidate is allowed to give his or her position on various issues. A moderator and panel of judges are often incorporated into the debate agenda. This will not be the case today." He paused to gather his thoughts and ensure that he had mentioned all he intended to say. He was still a bit uneasy knowing that some might accuse him and the school of crossing established boundaries where this issue was concerned. He continued.

"Now allow me to introduce you to two of our fine senior class members who will explain the format of tonight's presentations. Please help me welcome to the stage Senior Class President Barbara Robertson and Senior Class Vice-President Chris Fillmore." The two students enthusiastically approached the microphone as the audience gave them a hardy applause. Chris leaned over to the microphone before Barbara had a chance to speak. "Hi." This produced a chuckle from the crowd, especially among classmates. Barbara gave him a noticeably annoyed look as she nudged him aside.

"Hello. I'm Barbara." Again, the crowd reacted with a small laugh. "Oh, yeah, I guess you figured that out. Anyway, Chris and I are supposed to tell you how this works."

"Right." Chris once again hijacked the microphone.

Barbara gave Chris a look of displeasure. "That's why Chris is vice president and I'm president." The crowd once again responded in laughter. The heads of both students looked briefly to their right to see Principal Saunders give them a stern look of reprimand.

"So here we go," said Barbara as she looked down at the script. "Each presenter will first be given 25 minutes to present his or her position, beginning with Ms. Wagner."

It was now Chris's turn to speak. "Then each will have 15 minutes to respond, followed by a 10-minute wrap-up statement summarizing his or her position." He then added, "I guess they're trying to keep this short so you won't get too bored." Chris turned to see his school principal shake his head.

Barbara then continued. "Each presenter will be given a two-minute warning toward the end of their timed presentations. Now you might be wondering if we will allow questions after tonight's debate has concluded. The decision was made not to allow questions since it might take too much time. We could be here all night." She nodded to Chris.

"Oh, right." He looked down at his script but decided to use his own words rather than the ones before him. "Some of you might think the questions were rigged or get your feelings hurt." Chris enjoyed hearing the crowd's response to his humorous remark. He noticed the disapproving look from both Barbara and Mr. Saunders.

"Are you finished, Chris?" Barbara asked annoyingly. Chris nodded. "So I guess it's time to begin. Ms. Wagner and Mr. Provost, are you both ready?" Each gave an agreeable nod. "Then we will begin with Ms. Wagner." Barbara and Chris exited the stage as Clara Wagner approached the center microphone.

Clara Wagner's First Presentation

Clara was smartly dressed in a gray, tunic-length sweater and black, narrow pants. Her long, black hair fell gently over a magenta scarf loosely wrapped around her neck. She wore ankle boots rather than heels for comfort. The outfit worked well with her pear-shaped figure. Now at 44, she had earned the respect of her peers. She and her husband had been married for almost 20 years but had no children of their own. She found much satisfaction in teaching high school students. Clara was active in civic affairs and encouraged her students to do the same.

Clara set her tablet on the podium. She had carefully arranged her notes, expecting to refer to them only on brief occasions.

"It is an honor to stand before you today. As Principal Saunders said, Mr. Provost and I agreed to a debate. I am pleased that the school district allowed us to do so. So you might be wondering why evolution is taught in our schools and why it is recognized as a viable explanation for life on Earth. To begin with, we must be aware that most professional science institutions, with few exceptions, validate the truth of evolution. Please allow me to mention only a partial sample of these groups." Clara spent several minutes going through a list of respected and known entities that give credence to the science of evolution. In most cases, they state evolution as fact, not theory.

"So you see, when schools and courts and museums present evolution as fact, they do so upon the foundation of decades of well-established scientific analysis."

Clara asked the rhetorical question: "Why do these associations support evolution? The answer is simple. Science cannot and does not base conclusions upon the erroneous idea that any supernatural force is involved. Science must deal with the world and universe as it is. Science makes conclusions based upon the tools at our disposal. Evolution science must utilize material forces to explain life on Earth or anywhere else in the universe for that matter. Why would it ever factor in a religious point of view? Some who claim a creator God see evolution as a way to understand God's creation through the lens of science. The list of well-known Christians who support evolutionary science is significant. They affirm that God's creative power could have come through an evolutionary process. Some have pointed out that the Bible is not a science textbook."

Clara took a moment to mention the names, many of whom are well-known within Christian circles, from the past century up to the present day who conclude that evolution could be a viable method God used in His creation. She then shifted her emphasis.

"If someone points out inconsistencies within the evolutionary perspective, then what are we to do? Simply give up and go home?"

This statement prompted a laugh from the audience. "No. We examine the evidence and then move on. Perhaps mistakes have been made. Perhaps factors have yet to be discovered, especially when dealing with matters of antiquity. We adjust and readjust the analysis. The science of evolution is still . . . well . . . evolving." The crowd once again responded in laughter.

"Evolutionists admit that their theory is based upon both time and chance. It may have taken millions of years for one species to develop into another."

Clara spent the remaining time providing support for evolution. She began by mentioning the remarkable similarities between the skeletons of ancient four-limbed creatures and today's mammals. She spoke on the intermediate species of fossils such as the fossils of the oldest known whale species that appeared to have ears that later developed into a highly evolved hearing capability for modern whales. She mentioned an apparent whale fossil that appeared to be a land mammal with feet. She described as best she could without the benefit of visuals the similarities between ancient fossils and modern skeletal structures.

"Evolutionists have learned much by observing the variety of species on isolated islands such as Madagascar and Hawaii. In Madagascar, for instance, we find species found nowhere else on mainland continents. Lemurs are found only in Madagascar. But evolutionists can trace common ancestors on the mainland, dating from a time when there was a land bridge allowing ancient primates to cross over to Madagascar. A separate evolutionary ladder then began to emerge on the island."

Clara concluded her remarks and stated that she would address the genetic code in her next presentation. She sat down. Ron gave her a smile before standing up and moving to center stage. He wore a gray, tweed sports coat recently purchased solely for this event. Well-starched khaki slacks and a purple tie accompanied the jacket. He wanted to convey a hint of competency without appearing impersonal or rigid. Mona told him the tie gave him an air of aristocracy. He wasn't too sure he wanted to go that far. She then added, "But the jacket softens the royalty a bit." He would go with that.

Ron Provost's First Presentation

He carefully laid out his notes and then looked up at the audience. In his research, Ron had enough information to fill a textbook, but he realized he needed to confine his remarks to the allotted time.

"I first want you all to know that what I present to you tonight is not exhaustive. My purpose is to provide enough science as well as reasons why a creation science viewpoint is valid. I will also demonstrate why Darwinian evolution, or macroevolution, as it is sometimes called, is not factual science but wishful thinking by those who cling to the notion that it must be true even though the evidence reveals otherwise. Ms. Wagner pointed out the many scientific institutions and associations that support the evolutionary model. That is true. She also noted several Christian writers and theologians who hold to an evolutionary view. It is not my intention to denounce these institutions and supporters. What I will tell you is that quite a few scientists, biologists, paleontologists, and other scientific disciplines have begun to realize that the evidence does not substantiate the evolutionary model. Those who come out against evolution are often denounced for daring to speak against this long-held theory. Many have been censored, lost their jobs, or been barred from membership in various organizations. You see, the fact is that evolutionary theory is a colossal monster that has been swallowing up many of these scientific disciplines for decades. If you have been told all your life that evolution is a fact, then you begin to try to structure all your other belief systems to fit within that framework. Some of the Christian names Ms. Wagner mentioned are not scientists. They assume evolution is a proven science, so they adjust their thinking to fit that framework. I trust that what I reveal to you here tonight will cause you to rethink what has assaulted most of us throughout our lives."

Ron did not want to dwell too long on responding to Clara Wagner's presentation. In fact, he had not intended to counter Ms. Wagner's argument but decided he needed to provide another perspective on the matter. He found the place where he had left off in his notes and continued.

"By demonstrating why evolution is not possible, I will consequently demonstrate why creation is the only viable explanation for life on Earth. I want to encourage you all to investigate further these matters, for the implications of this issue will have a far-reaching impact on how you view life on Earth in general and your own life in particular. How we view the world determines the values we hold and the choices we make. So with that said, I'll get started."

Ron decided to open with the subject of DNA due to the abundance of attention being given to the effect it has had on evolutionary theory.

"Let me begin by addressing that tiny molecule carried by every living organism. I'm referring to DNA, which is a shortened reference to deoxyribonucleic acid. You've probably heard of DNA in reference to how it has helped law enforcement identify victims and criminal offenders. I'm going to take us further into the particulars of this molecule. Much of the science of DNA came about in the mid-20th century. It was discovered that DNA provided information regarding the genetic makeup of all living things in addition to other functions within every organism. In other words, it is not the chemical properties or shape of this DNA molecule but the language or code it bears that determines the makeup of every living organism on Earth, which, of course, includes you and me. But before I get into this further, let me point out that evolutionary theory is based on two main principles. One of those is called natural selection. And wouldn't you know, as it turns out, natural selection is an observable fact. It explains how, for instance, one species of the canine genus can be bred through multiple generations to create a great diversity in breeds of dogs, wolves, coyotes, dingoes, and every other canine throughout the world. However, macroevolution states that one type of mammal evolved from another genus of mammals, such as a mouse evolving into a bat or primate or bear or, yes, eventually you and me. The evolutionist would not necessarily agree with the chronology I just mentioned, but they do assert that natural selection will eventually result in a crossover of one classification of a living thing to another given enough time and the element of random chance. The classifications under the animal kingdom include, starting at the top, phylum and then class, order, family, genus, and species. The plant kingdom has other names of classifications, but for our purposes, we will deal only with the animal kingdom. Any animal within a classification above genus has never been observed to cross over into another classification. Evolutionists admit this but tell us that it did occur millions of years ago.

"The other principle of evolution is based on mutations within the genome of living organisms. This principle is absolutely foundational to the tenets of evolutionary theory. I will eventually speak a little more about mutations, but for now, I want to continue with more facts concerning the function of the DNA molecule.

"It is this DNA molecule that provides the blueprint for life. It is made up of units called genes. Each gene determines a specific characteristic of your body, such as eye color or the shape of your face, gender, and, in fact, every aspect of what makes you distinct from every other living person. I find it marvelous to think that DNA can have literally billions if not trillions of variations within the history of the human race. Each human DNA molecule is about two meters in length. Try to wrap your mind around that. This roughly six-foot strand is found in almost every cell of your body. Each strand contains over three billion pairs of nucleotides. Don't concern yourself too much with what a nucleotide is. Just know that scientists give the four types of nucleotides a letter designation of either A, T, C, or G. These codes, in combination, make up a language. Think of the combination of these four codes as letters in a book. It has been noted that the human DNA code is equivalent to over 200 King James Bibles. Each three-letter combination codes an amino acid. The amino acids form proteins. Proteins form living cells. Our body is made up of roughly 100 trillion cells. If I were able to show you an actual or computerized animation sequence of the process of DNA replication along with the activity of proteins within the human cell, it would appear as an assembly line or, rather, a manufacturing plant. It is an amazing thing to witness. Sometimes the nucleotides can mutate. That means a base nucleotide within the DNA sequence is changed. The vast numbers of mutations are detrimental to living organisms and can create abnormalities or disease, but these mutations are thought to also help animals or plants adapt to different environments. Herein lies the foundation for evolutionary theory. More often, however, the process of natural selection is explained another way. Let me give you an illustration. Let's say that you have a long-necked giraffe that mates with another long-necked giraffe. However, both the giraffes contain a short-necked gene. They live in an environment where there are tall trees with limbs up high. The female has a calf born with a short neck because its DNA contained the short-necked gene from both parents. The calf got the 'short end of the gene,' so to speak. As the calf grows, it is unable to reach the high leaves of the tree. It does not survive. That means the short-necked gene will eventually be removed from the gene pool within the colony. This may not be the best example, but the same kind of thing happens continually within every classification of living things. This process has nothing to do with mutations.

"Let's dig a little deeper. When molecular scientists first viewed the structure of the DNA molecule, they found that it wasn't just some random structure or an elusive component of the cell but that it had an actual language. As I mentioned earlier, the code of information determines the very identity and unique trait of every living thing. The arrangement of the code is still a mystery. DNA needs proteins and enzymes to create DNA. But you need DNA to make the proteins and enzymes. So to emphasize, DNA is like a computer software program that is written into each cell of your body. Keep this in mind. DNA contains a language. This language is not a random set of codes. It is a precise blueprint for the makeup of every living thing.

"Darwin noted that it was 'absurd in the highest degree' to suppose that the human eye evolved through natural selection. In all fairness to Mr. Darwin, he then added, 'The difficulty of believing that a perfect and complex eye could be formed by natural selection, though insuperable by our imagination, should not be considered subversive of the theory.'[1] He still believed his theory was valid.

"Before we make too much of this, I will tell you that evolutionary researchers made a new discovery. They studied a marine worm that resembles fossils of an ancient ancestor. They noticed that the shape of the worm's brain resembled rods and cones in the human eye. This was a great aha moment for evolutionists. Finding a similar cell structure between the worm's brain and the human eye led them to state firmly that there was common evolutionary ancestry. Yes, they hypothesized that the human eye has an evolutionary origin common to that of a worm brain." A chuckle was heard throughout the crowd. "In fact, the eye of almost every living creature contains cones and rods, but the evolutionist looks at an ancient fossil resembling a marine worm and interprets it to mean our eyes had their origin from a worm brain. This, ladies and gentlemen, demonstrates how far the evolutionist will go to lend support to their theory, stating to the world that it is not theory but fact. They do so because they are convinced that random changes brought about the complex and orderly life on our planet without the benefit of a Creator. They are so convinced of this that they simply ignore the evidence of an intelligent Creator. If we see the design in our world, many evolutionists would say that it simply gives an *appearance* of design.

"Let me also state that the complexity of the human eye does not hold a candle to the complex structure of the DNA molecule. Darwin, of course, knew little of the microscopic world. Since Darwin's day, great scientific advances have allowed us to see further into the DNA and RNA molecules, as well as other microscopic organisms. If he knew more of this unseen world, would he have continued to advance his theory? We can only speculate. But because he did so, he is now held in high esteem. Perhaps this is due in part because his theories gave so many excuses to ignore or doubt the Creator's design.

"I want to drive home the point that DNA contains a six-billion letter code that provides the assembly instructions for making . . . well . . . you. Every single living thing has DNA. I mentioned RNA. RNA is similar to DNA. It is involved in the replication of DNA."

Ron Provost went on to describe the structure and function of DNA molecules, describing their twisted, ladder-type structure and the components of nucleotides, codons, genes, and chromosomes, which, when combined, provide the language and genomes for what it takes to give us our unique identities. He explained the structure and function of the RNA molecule. He then described the many functions of proteins, emphasizing the tiny parts of the cell and how proteins help maintain and drive all the tiny and varied machines within the cell. Ron related these processes to that of an aircraft manufacturing procedure from the formation of design all the way through to the construction of a high-performance aircraft.

"The complex language that provides the information for an assembly line process from DNA, RNA, and proteins would make the most ingenious engineer envious of this engineering marvel. In fact, chances are that even the most intelligent person in the world would not have been able to dream up such a wondrous process as this. And oh, by the way, this process is multiplied literally trillions of times within your body in order to ensure that your body performs as it should. Creationists and evolutionists both agree that all these microscopic entities are incredibly versatile and complex machines. The enigma for the evolutionist is this: Where did all this information come from? Creationists propose the answer. It came from the mind of a divine Creator."

Ron again scanned his audience. He knew he was merely scratching the surface of such a wondrous subject and was hoping that many in the crowd were absorbing this information. He was hoping that those who were on the fence concerning this issue would be in agreement with him that all of this pointed to the wonders of a divine Creator who was beyond our ability to imagine or comprehend.

"There is a debate within evolutionary circles as to which came first—protein or RNA. You see, it takes RNA to replicate DNA, which in turn produces proteins. You can't make new proteins without RNA, and you can't make new DNA without proteins. So which came first, proteins or RNA? I'm sure I may have confused you, but rather than go back and try to explain this further, let's move on. Even the most ardent evolutionists will admit that DNA with its complex language and RNA, a necessary tool in replicating DNA, are incredibly complex machines that could not have emerged suddenly on the microbiological scene without the benefit of some unknown factor. Adding to this is the fact that proteins are quite fragile. The protein factory must continue to pump out more and more in order to manage the task set before them of assembling you and me.

"So, we now have the proverbial question of which came first—the chicken or the egg? Proteins or RNA? Evolutionists continue to wrestle with this problem, supposing that the RNA molecule could replicate itself and thus overcome the need for proteins. Another obstacle must be overcome. This self-replicating activity needs energy. Where did it come from? The evolutionists are hard at work trying to find solutions to these and other nagging questions.

"I will not continue down this road of speculation and scientific head-scratching. Suffice it to say that the evolutionists will propose many complex reasons why all these obstacles were overcome in the distant past, speculating on possible processes and entities that no longer exist or that have yet to be discovered. Lots of time, money, and energy are spent on trying to find a workable solution. Do I fault them for continuing down this road of discovery? Not at all. This is what science does. We, humans, are always searching for answers. My complaint does not lie with continued scientific evolutionary research. My complaint is with lawyers and courts, governmental entities, museums, and politicians who try to silence other views, and even the scientific basis for those views, for the origin of life. Educators like me teach the material we are mandated to teach. We are on the periphery of this debate. Educators and students alike are crippled and even shackled for being denied other perspectives on this topic that may very well be the most significant scientific and philosophical question of all time. Where did we come from, and why are we here?

"Call us simpletons if you like, but creationists have the answer. It took and still takes an intelligent, all-knowing Creator. Random chance over eons of time will never produce these marvels of engineering. The evolutionist simply will not and, I might add, cannot accept this solution. Their presupposed bias will not allow them to consider anything other than a naturalistic cause. We creationists begin with the premise that something did not come from nothing in a purely naturalistic universe.

It took an intelligent being from outside the bounds of the known universe, and there is the science to back up that presupposition."

Ron looked up from his notes to determine if his audience was still with him. All eyes, or at least the faces on the first few rows, were still on him. This provided him the encouragement and confidence to continue. He looked down at his watch and noticed he still had a few minutes to continue his first presentation. After a brief pause, he looked down at his notes and continued.

"Let us now direct our attention to the fossil record. We are led to believe that fossils provide proof of evolution. In fact, the opposite is true.

"Darwin stated that, over time, fossils would emerge, proving his hypothesis. They never did so. Oh, to be sure, evolutionists will point to this fossil or that fossil and suggest it denotes a stage of evolutionary development. Time and time again this has proven not to be the case. Darwin's theory proposes slow changes over long periods of time. Instead, the fossil record actually reveals a vast variety of fossils over a short period of time, none of which were transitional in form."

Ron attempted to describe the structure of geologic periods that allow paleontologists to correlate time to layers of sedimentary rocks. He knew he had a limited amount of time and did not want to lose his audience on such mundane material. He was beginning to wish he and Clara had allowed themselves the use of visuals. He tried to make this segment of his presentation short, but he also realized that without this knowledge, he would not be able to state clearly the evidence for the lack of transitional fossils.

"Let me just say that . . ."

He was interrupted by Barbara, the senior class president. "Mr. Provost, you have two minutes remaining."

Ron thought for a moment. He was about to get into a subject that needed to be kept intact.

"I will end now and allow my opponent's response."

Barbara was caught off guard and looked to Principal Saunders for direction. He nodded, indicating she should move on. "Ms. Wagner? Are you ready to present your second segment?"

"Yes, Barbara. Thank you." Clara passed Ron as they traded places. Both avoided eye contact.

Clara Wagner's Second Presentation

Clara knew Ron would use DNA in his arsenal of objections to evolution. She was ready to refute his claims.

"Mr. Provost had a great deal to say about DNA, the genetic code that makes up all living organisms. What he failed to mention is that this genetic code that is common among all living things is just that; it is common among all living things. Why is that? It is because we all come from common ancestry. We see common traits among all mammals, for instance. Mr. Provost mentioned that one necessary component of evolution is mutations within the genetic code. This is true. Let me provide an illustration. It was discovered several centuries ago that humans needed vitamin C to survive. Seafarers noted that sailors were contracting scurvy, which resulted in many deaths onboard these long voyages. They needed outside sources of vitamin C, whereas the animals onboard such as horses and dogs did not. We humans do not have the enzymes needed to synthesize vitamin C. Evolutionists also found that other primates such as chimpanzees, monkeys, and gorillas also do not have this enzyme within their genetic makeup. Evolution has the answer. At one point in the distant past, an early ancestor of all primates and humans did, indeed, have this enzyme. A mutation caused the further line of evolutionary ancestry to be without this enzyme that produces vitamin C. We need oranges and other citric fruit to allow us to go on living. This is not the case for earlier versions on the evolutionary tree of life."

Clara continued to mention the family tree of evolutionary science. She pointed out the obvious pattern of skeletal and other body systems that developed over millions of years.

Clara turned her attention once again to the fossil record. "Fossils cannot prove that one species crossed over into another species. What the fossil record shows us are many slight modifications from one type of fossil to another. What we can conclude from this is that an evolutionary process must have been involved.

"When scientists viewed the various layers of earth and rock, they noted that more advanced fossils were near the top layer, while older and more primitive fossils were near the bottom."

Clara then turned her attention to the other proponent of evolutionary theory—natural selection. She pointed out that natural selection provides adaptive change, unlike genetic variations that must rely on chance. She spoke of the conditions that would result in one species crossing over into what we would now call a separate species.

Barbara gave Ms. Wagner her two-minute warning. Clara spent her final two minutes pulling together all the evidence she had mentioned in order to emphasize the abundance of evidence for evolution being considered factual science.

Ron once again waited for Clara to sit before he stood and made his way to center stage.

Ron Provost's Second Presentation

"I was about to get into the topic of the fossil record. So I'll pick up where I left off." He took a breath and exhaled slowly.

"There's another story in the rock layers that does not support evolutionary theory. In fact, even today it mystifies many evolutionists. The Cambrian time period reveals an interesting event that paleontologists have named the Cambrian Explosion. Even as far back as the mid to late 19th century, geologists and paleontologists have been studying the fossil record found in this Cambrian layer of sedimentary rock. Charles Darwin himself found this event to be quite remarkable. For here in the Earth's strata were many unique and diverse marine fossils, all apparently living side by side. Many of these life forms are now extinct. What evolutionists have been searching for over the past 150 years are fossils of the proposed transitional life forms. Instead, what they have found is an actual explosion of completely unique life forms that seemed to have appeared suddenly over a short span of time. This puzzled Darwin and still continues to puzzle many paleontologists and evolutionists today.

Instead of Darwin's proposed evolutionary branching tree illustration of less advanced life forms at the bottom of the tree branching off into more complex life forms, the Cambrian period reveals more of an orchard of a wide variety of life forms all appearing at once. No intermediate or transitional fossils were found."

Ron briefly described the proposed reasons evolutionists give as to why these transitional forms were absent from the record.

"Other fossil finds produce the same outcome—no transitional forms. For instance, the Burgess shale reveals even more animal forms but lacks precursor forms.

"One paleontologist, Samuel Bowring from MIT, made the statement, 'We now know how fast, fast is,' and then added, 'What I like to ask my biologist friends is, How fast can evolution get before they start feeling uncomfortable?'[2] The discomfort comes from the discovery of just how fast the transition from one ancestral form to another must have taken place. Do they still continue to call it evolution? In fairness to the evolutionists, they continue to debate among themselves the mechanisms that must have taken place to explain the sudden explosion of diverse life forms within a short period of time. Their preconceived bias will not allow them to deny an evolutionary model. The experts wonder if genetic mutations and natural selection are the only two foundations upon which evolutionary theory stands. They keep wondering, 'What are we missing?' Ask creationists. They can provide the answer.

"Evolutionists talk a lot about time and chance. Scientists and mathematicians, too, have hypothesized the amount of time it would take for there to be the number and kinds of mutations and natural selections and intermediate changes to occur from the earliest life forms up through today's more advanced forms. The results reveal that the 3.5 billion years evolutionists claim from the origin of life on Earth to the present day is not enough time for all these changes to occur. And again, these intermediate changes are not showing up in the fossil record.

"Still, evolutionists argue that there are no weaknesses in evolutionary theory. They will not acknowledge any other theory or perspective.

"Now, let's talk about sex." Ron joined the audience in laughter. "Perhaps I'd better use the word reproduction instead." Again, a chuckle came from the crowd.

"The reproductive component continues to baffle evolutionists. Less complex life forms reproduce in a much different way than more advanced life forms do. Evolutionists will admit that in today's world, an animal from one genus can't mate with an animal from another genus classification. For instance, a member of the primate family cannot mate with a member of the feline family to produce another unique form of life. What is the explanation given by evolutionists for this mystery? The solution has yet to be discovered, they will say. Okay, then, we'll concede the point that an unknown factor is at play here.

"Each living organism has a unique DNA molecule that contains a completely unique code. This language manufactures specific kinds of proteins. For one living organism to evolve into another kind of living organism outside of its own species, it needs a completely unique set of DNA codes. To give you an example, let's say you want to change the words from the book *A Tale of Two Cities* by Charles Dickens into *Great Expectations* by the same author. Can the letters and words of the first book be rearranged to form the new book? That would be highly unlikely, but let's explore that proposition a little further. Both books were written only two years apart and by the very same author. Surely some of the same style and vernacular were used. One book has slightly more pages than the other. Perhaps a few more letters and words were added. Could you still create one book from the same letters and words of the other? I would have to say that yes, perhaps it could happen. But what would it take to do that? Random chance? No. It would take an intelligent being to accomplish such a task. My point is this: The evolutionist can show us fossils of what appears to be a whale with limbs and then compare it to what we now recognize as a whale. They will suggest that the four-legged supposed 'whale' evolved into an aquatic version of that land mammal. But what they fail to explain is how the DNA code that would be required not only to develop flippers from limbs but to completely rearrange cell structure, tendons, ligaments, nervous system, and brain function with newly formed neurotransmitters, stimuli to the muscles, new muscle formation, and . . . well, you get the point. They might then bring up the fact that both apparently breathe air. How about that? So whales must have evolved from land mammals. Correct? That's quite a stretch given that elusive and problematic little molecule known as DNA. We are forced to continue to come back to that messy, complicating factor.

"We also must continually come back to the driving force behind the Darwinian evolutionary theory, which says that evolution occurs from a combination of mutations and natural selection. What this foundational theory does not explain is where the information comes from in these new evolutionary forms. You see, mutations do not explain how completely new information is developed. Mutations might change a code letter here and there within the DNA code language. But it does not create newly developed code or language."

"Mr. Provost, you have two minutes left." This time it was Chris Fillmore who noted the remaining time.

Ron looked at his watch that he had placed on the platform. He knew he had but two minutes left. He decided to nail down his point about the need for new information in the supposed evolutionary mechanism. He quoted a well-known creationist whose books have brought up problems with evolutionary theory. This author, lecturer, and advocate of intelligent design mentioned the mathematical improbability of a rearrangement of the DNA code necessary to create functional proteins by random chance alone, even over eons of time. Here is where Ron would need the benefit of visuals to fully explain these calculations and provide illustrations that would drive home his point. He chose to skim over this section. He made sure he would complete his final remarks in the given time after Clara completed her wrap-up.

Ron concluded his remarks. "Thank you for your time."

"And now we will hear Ms. Wagner's closing remarks," announced Barbara.

Clara Wagner's Closing Remarks

For this segment of her presentation, Clara chose not to bring her tablet to the podium. She had this segment nailed down in her mind.

"Thank you once again for attending tonight's event. It is a topic that apparently will never be fully resolved since we are speaking of things from our ancient past. And so the debate continues."

Clara opened by reiterating the many notable institutions and associations that had given their full support of evolution. "Quite frankly, the synthesis for evolution is shifting somewhat. There are new discoveries about life on Earth such as why some people are prone to genetic disorders while others are not or why pesticides sooner or later fail to keep those pesky pests in check. The modern synthesis for evolution takes into account the effect behavior and the environment have on the future evolutionary process. It has always been the case that when a new scientific discovery is made, subsequent discoveries may alter or change how we view the original. On a molecular level, biologists have noted how changes in the environment cause cellular changes, often resulting in the shutdown of certain genes. Did I lose you? In a way, I hope so. You see, we must often leave it up to those experts in various fields of study to do the difficult research. While evolutionary science still stands behind the two legs of support—mutations through chance and natural selection over eons of time—the bigger picture still continues to emerge with each new scientific discovery. Fossils continue to be unearthed. Scientists are finding that climate change in the past had a profound effect upon the development of Homo sapiens and our early ancestors."

Clara then shifted her focus to modern laboratory experiments that observe the change in microbes from each subsequent generation to the next. She continued. "In order to demonstrate the process of macroevolution, scientists are observing the changes that take place from one generation of microbes to the next. Since these generational changes occur more rapidly than other more advanced organisms, they have detected what appear to be newly developed species. So you see, even in this modern age, we have demonstrated the very process of macroevolution."

She brought her presentation to a close. "I hope I have convinced you by scientific reasoning that you can place your faith in evolutionary science over the unscientific explanation given by creationists. What is their explanation? They claim that every living organism merely came into existence from the finger-snap of a supernatural power."

Clara walked slowly back to her chair.

Chris rose from his seat and announced, "And now Mr. Provost will deliver his final presentation."

Ron Provost's Closing Remarks

Ron silently prayed and thanked the Lord for the opportunity he had been given. He asked that the Lord give him the peace, confidence, and sound mind to deliver his closing argument. He walked to the microphone.

"Science teaches us that a hypothesis must be testable and repeatable. Asking us to accept evolution as fact when it can do neither is dishonest. Claiming that evolution is verifiable science while stating that creation science is not science at all, claiming that it has been tested and shown to be wrong is a misrepresentation of both evolution and creation science. I have offered you only a few reasons why creation science is a more viable explanation for the origin and progression of life on Earth. There is much more I could have brought before you this evening."

Ron thought for a moment.

"Well . . . I am going to take a chance that I have time to mention this other factor. I am going to talk about Earth itself. I wish I had time to mention the many factors that came together to support life on this planet. There are upwards of 20 different factors that must be present simultaneously in order to generate and sustain life on our planet.[3] Some researchers maintain that to have a planet that will sustain complex life as we know it on Earth, well, the probability is one in one quadrillionth chance. We all must admit that this is well beyond our ability to comprehend. We must compare that to the estimated 100 billion stars in our galaxy alone. Probability is something science must always consider.

The likelihood of all these probable factors coming together at once is out of the realm of likelihood even when considering the billions of galaxies in the known universe. This compels us to consider the probable cause as coming from a divine Creator who would have created the Earth and the consequential life it produces for, dare I say, a grand purpose."

Ron took a deep breath. He wanted to make sure his final remarks were adequately conveyed. This would be his final chance to point his audience to the Creator of all things.

"Ms. Wagner and I have both expressed to you the fact that evolution counts on time along with random chance to account for the progression of life on Earth. I would like to add this: Evolution requires, in fact, *purposeless* changes to substantiate its claims. Did you catch that? I said purposeless changes. Let me put it to you this way. Each of you has no real purpose for being here."

Ron paused for emphasis. "Or at least as far as evolution is concerned. You see, the only way for anything to have a purpose is if someone gives it that purpose. The etymology, or origin, of the term *purpose*, came from a word that meant 'intention, aim, goal, or the reason for which something exists.' You cannot grant it a purpose solely based on what it accomplishes or how it functions. For instance, there are many different systems and functions within the human body working in harmony, which allow our bodies to work.

"I want to speak once again about the function of the human eye, which fascinated Charles Darwin. It is made up of 10 general components, all working simultaneously to give you sight. I would suggest that the human eye has a purpose and not just a function. Its purpose is to give you a view of your environment, which then allows you to function within that same environment. If I may, I will also add what I believe to be an even greater purpose for the human eye. It allows us to see and then marvel at the creation surrounding us. In today's world, we have the privilege of viewing images from the deepest abyss of the ocean floor. From the Hubble and James Webb telescopes, we are now able to see out into the far reaches of the universe. Sophisticated microscopes allow us to see down to the tiniest known microscopic particles. We can view the beauty of a sunset. We see the diversity of earthly terrains, plants, animals, and peoples of the world. We are able to study just how harmonious and synchronous life is on our planet and even within the entire universe. So what's the purpose of all of this? Evolutionists tell us that none of this has any purpose. They tell us that purpose and design behind the purpose is but an illusion."

Ron once again paused briefly to allow that statement to settle in his audience's minds. He wondered if those in the hearing of his voice might challenge his supposition or consider his presentation to go beyond scientific analysis. He was confident he had crossed no barriers. On top of that was the fact that the school board had approved his entire presentation.

"Please allow me to wax philosophical. The purpose of eyesight, as well as insight for that matter, is for you and I to be in awe of not just creation itself but of the very One who created it. I will confidently propose that this is the purpose behind creation. Consider this: Evolution cannot explain purpose. It can only explain function. Science can explain how and why you and I function. It might even suggest your function within society. However, science alone will never give you the answer to your ultimate purpose for being on this Earth.

"Let's suppose you go to an art museum. While pursuing the halls of art, your eyes are directed to a certain painting. You become fixated on that painting. It is beautiful. The painting is so mesmerizing and beautiful that you are taken with the image it conveys. You begin to speculate on the story behind the painting. You become emotional and even shed a tear as you stare at it in wonder. For a brief moment in time, you become immersed in the essence of this work of art. What is happening here? The one who designed and created the painting did so to perhaps bring about an emotional response from the viewer. You didn't look at the painting and wonder about the chemical makeup of the paint or the composition of the canvas mat or what type of device was used to apply those chemical compounds to the mat. You didn't measure the dimensions of the frame. No. The painter gave that painting a purpose. While the painting itself is remarkable and beautiful, the ultimate purpose of it is to direct you to the one who created it. We give honor to Rembrandt, Monet, Goya, Van Gogh, and Picasso. Why does evolution deny that we give honor to the One who designed, created, and gave beauty to you and me, or to any other created thing? For sure, some evolutionists will try to say that the method the grand Creator used in His creation was evolution but will continue to ignore any mention of His creative hand and minimize other accounts such as the evidence for the origin of life in Scripture. They suppress the truth as they give high honor to their evolutionary theories that they guard with defiance.

"The appearance of design isn't just a common-sense factor; it comes from a scientific explanation to which I have spoken here tonight.

"Each one of you has the ability to hear, read, study, and think about everything that goes into your mind. While we do well to consider objective theory, we still must then decide for ourselves what it is we are going to believe. We are not just lab rats responding to stimuli. We can reason, love, express emotions, think deeply on matters, and create things—not just as an evolutionary function but from our innate giftedness and developed talents.

"Give much consideration to what is true. Consider what is splendid and beautiful and magnificent. Think about things that are right or lovely or worthy of your admiration. Reflect on those things, not just as some facts of science but on the effect these things have on your very heart and soul. There is a word for those thoughts and feelings that penetrate deep within the depths of your soul. The word is *visceral*. No other creature on this privileged terrestrial ball has this ability. Visceral feelings are not merely a product of our DNA or the chemical and electrical impulses within our brain. Evolution offers no explanation for these deeply rooted expressions of artistic and creative thoughts and ideas. These things come from our Creator. May we not merely skim the surface of wisdom and knowledge without ever going deep. These things are meant to propel you to a deeper awareness of the world around you. They are even meant to propel us to the eternal realm."

Principal Saunders nervously glanced at the timer in front of the two students. Barbara missed her queue. Saunders tapped her on the shoulder.

"Oh, oh, my goodness. I'm sorry, Mr. Provost. I was supposed to give you your two-minute warning. Um, it looks like you have a little less than a minute."

"That's okay, Barbara. I'm finished. I will just repeat that what I have presented to you this evening is a mere fraction of the scientific basis for an intelligent Creator. I also suggest very strongly that each of you consider your ultimate purpose within creation and then realize that evolution cannot and does not provide any real purpose for being alive."

A momentary awkward pause was followed by escalating applause from the audience. Ron felt uneasy, realizing he may have ended on a downbeat. Still, he was hopeful that his presentation had caused many to consider the perspective and viability of a Creator for the origin of life, as well as that of the Creator's ultimate special creation—all of mankind.

Principal Saunders walked back on stage and motioned for Clara to join Ron at center stage. The audience continued their applause intermixed with accolades and cheers. Principal Saunders, along with Clara and Ron, invited the two students to join them at center stage, resulting in an uproar among the students in the audience.

One particular former student in the audience was taking notes, but not of the presentations. She was writing down reasons why Ron Provost might be a good choice for the Thought Transmission study. Nora Bernard texted her boss, "I have the perfect candidate."

CHAPTER 11

MONDAY AFTERNOON, NOVEMBER 22, 2027
RON PROVOST'S CLASSROOM AT
FREEBURG HIGH SCHOOL

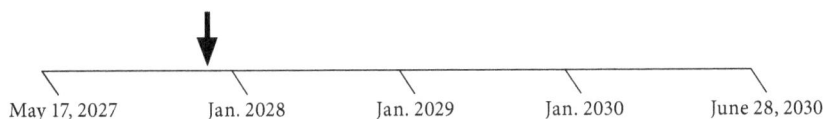

		↓			
May 17, 2027	Jan. 2028	Jan. 2029	Jan. 2030	June 28, 2030

The school bell rang as Ron Provost sat at his classroom desk taking advantage of his break by checking emails. It was the Monday after Friday's debate. Several students passed by the open door and stuck their heads in.

"Mr. Provost, you rock," said one. "Way to go, Mr. Provost," said another. Several other students offered similar remarks.

Ron had already received hundreds of emails. He took a sip of coffee. He placed his left elbow on the table and a clenched fist under his chin. The other hand maneuvered the mouse as he glanced through the comments. They ran the gamut from encouragement and even adoration to castigation. In either case, he realized he had touched a nerve. He took another sip of coffee just as the classroom phone rang. He was hoping it would be a pleasant call rather than additional inflammatory comments from a few.

He set his coffee down and answered. "Ron Provost."

"Mr. Provost, my name is Nora Bernard. I was a student of yours several years back, and I was at the debate last Friday evening."

"Yes."

"Anyway, I'm not here to comment on the debate, but rather . . ."

Ron interrupted her. "Oh, Nora Bernard. Yes, I remember you."

"You do?"

"Yes, of course. You were one of my best students, Nora. What can I do for you?"

Nora was relieved to hear receptive words coming from her former teacher. "Well, after high school, I went on to study various sciences at King's University in Toronto. I ended up concentrating my studies in the field of neuroscience and now work for one of the professors at the university."

"Oh, that's wonderful, Nora. Sounds fascinating. So what prompted you to call me?" Ron was curious.

"After the debate, I contacted my boss about inviting you to participate in a study we're conducting. After I told her about you, she agreed that you might be a good candidate."

"What kind of study?"

Nora had anticipated the question but was still uncertain how to answer given the confidential nature of the study. "It has to do with how the brain reacts to thoughts."

"Okay." Ron could tell that Nora was not being forthright with her words. "Go on . . ."

Nora considered her response and then added, "Well, you would be paid for your participation, which would only be a part-time or occasional use of your time." Nora was fumbling for the right words to speak. This was her only chance to gain his trust and interest.

"You're holding back. I can tell."

"Yes, Mr. Provost. You see, this is a groundbreaking study, and the team decided it should be held in the strictest confidence. In other words, Mr. Provost, I can't tell you too much at this time, but I really believe you would be a great asset, and you would be paid well for . . ."

Ron interrupted her. "Hang on, Nora." Ron made some quick observations. "I am honored that you would consider me for what is apparently a worthwhile study, but I really need to know more before I can give you an answer."

"Of course, Mr. Provost." Nora slowed her words down and continued. "I . . . I mean we weren't expecting an answer from you right away. What we are asking of you at this time is to give Dr. Myers a visit, and she can provide you with more answers and get a sense of whether you and the study are a good match."

"Who is Dr. Myers?"

"Oh, I'm sorry. Dr. Suzanne Myers is my boss. She is the one who initiated the study. She formed a team, and now we are recruiting paid volunteers."

"If I agree to meet with your boss, I am going to need to let my wife know what is going on. So how often would you need me, and, may I ask, how much does it pay?"

Nora gave Ron a rundown of the proposed schedule and mentioned that he would only be needed occasionally when certain experiments were run. She then mentioned the compensation.

"What?" Ron was surprised at the enormous amount that would be paid for such a limited amount of his time. "And where would these experiments be conducted?"

Nora realized she had finally grabbed his interest. "At the university." She then added, "Honestly, we are not quite sure just how often you would be asked to come in. We can adjust our schedule to yours to some degree." Nora wanted to make sure Ron Provost knew the significance of the study and his participation in it. "Mr. Provost, I want you to know that the nature of this study is no small thing. If we are successful, it would change the course of scientific and medical understanding of how and why the brain functions as it does." She paused briefly. "And how individuals who suffer from brain dysfunction might be helped." Nora was trying to be cautious but also engaging with the words she used. "And I want to let you know, Mr. Provost, that I remember how you treated your students. I remembered how well you stayed on point in your teachings. You were concise and made the material easy to understand. You explained everything so well. And Mr. Provost, you had a profound influence on my own decision to study science. When I heard about the debate, I wanted to come and hear your side of the controversy because I know you give a lot of thought to what you say."

Ron allowed Nora to complete her words and then spoke up. "Thank you for the compliment, Nora. And I can tell that you really believe in what your boss—Dr. Myers is it? —is trying to accomplish. So, here's what I'll do. Let me talk this over with my wife, Mona, and get back to you by this time tomorrow. Is that all right?"

Nora was delighted to hear her former teacher's response. She gave him her phone number as well as Dr. Myers' office number. They finished up the phone call with a few pleasantries, especially fond memories from Nora's former days at Freeburg High School.

"Good to hear from you, Nora. You have my word I will call you this time tomorrow."

"Thank you, Mr. Provost. Bye."

Ron could not imagine what this mysterious study was all about but was certainly curious enough to give it serious consideration.

CHAPTER 12

JUNE 11, 2030
GENEVA SCIENCE CONFERENCE
SEVERAL MINUTES INTO DR. SUZANNE
MYERS' PRESENTATION

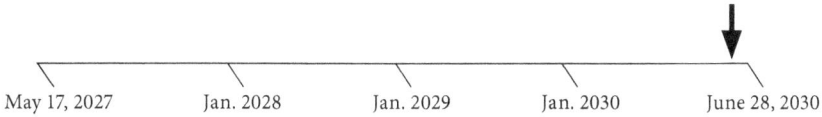

May 17, 2027   Jan. 2028   Jan. 2029   Jan. 2030   June 28, 2030

As Dr. Suzanne Myers introduced the team members from the Thought Transmission study to the conference crowd, they were given a moment to relate their participation and perspectives on the merits of the project.

Suzanne rose from her seat on the stage to join over 2,000 attendees in showing their appreciation for the work each team member had contributed to the Thought Transmission project. As the applause subsided, Suzanne walked once more to the microphone and continued her presentation.

"Now once again it is my pleasure to introduce to you several volunteers, who without their willingness to be our guinea pigs . . ." (a collective laugh came from the crowd), "we would not have been able to achieve success." Suzanne attempted to control her emotions. "While we had several volunteers, only three were able to join us today. Two of these, Kiara Patel and Anthony Schumacher, you will hear from in our afternoon session led by Dr. Randal Milton. You will hear from Ron Provost, our other volunteer, further on in this morning's presentation."

Photos of each volunteer were shown on the screens as Dr. Myers related several attributes each volunteer brought to the study. Her voice quavered, revealing considerable affection and appreciation she had for each volunteer.

"I would like to mention one particular volunteer whose determination and dedication continued even after our study encountered several setbacks. I am speaking of Erin Roberts who was unable to join us here today due to her work schedule. Despite the setbacks we encountered, Erin's tenacity allowed us to overcome obstacles and make adjustments. That allowed us to learn and change, which eventually brought us success. In addition to Erin's tenacity, she also demonstrated commitment and devotion to not just this study but also to the people in her life. There is one other quality we found to be true of Erin Roberts. She did not see her involvement in our project as a mere job but as a pioneering opportunity. For you see, Erin Roberts has the heart of an adventurer."

CHAPTER 13

MAY 22, 2028
SILHOUETTE TRAIL INSIDE KILLARNEY
PROVINCIAL PARK ONTARIO, CANADA

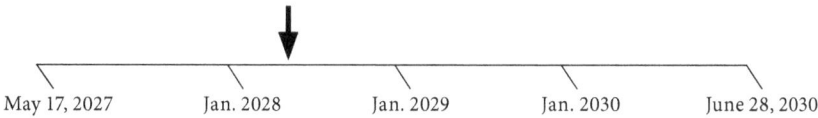

↓

| May 17, 2027 | Jan. 2028 | Jan. 2029 | Jan. 2030 | June 28, 2030 |

Three hikers were nearing Three Narrows Lake. It had been two days since leaving their George Lake campsite near the Killarney Provincial Park office. Erin Roberts, Katelyn Price, and Tamara Toussaint had been preparing for this excursion since February. Erin and Katelyn had taken leave from their job at the Royal Canadian Mint in Ontario. Tamara took leave from her work as a correctional officer in Ottawa. In addition to her job at the Mint, Erin had applied and been accepted to the Thought Transmission study several months back. The team had agreed to her upcoming hike under the condition that she keep her knowledge of the study in strictest confidence. Now in May, the weather was perfect for their two-week adventure. They set out on Saturday, May 20, 2028, to hike the Silhouette Trail.

Erin Roberts was the more experienced hiker. Her swarthy complexion came from the many outdoor activities she pursued. Experience and confidence made her the envy of her two hiking companions. "See? Do you see what I mean? Crystal clear blue. Right?" Erin was excited to share this sight with her two companions as they rounded the ridge overlooking the lake.

"So that's Topaz Lake. Would you look at that!" Katelyn was impressed. "It's even more stunning than I imagined."

"Beautiful. God be praised. It is easy to see why it is named Topaz." Tamara spoke through labored breathing. She was less fit than the others but was keeping pace nevertheless.

"Maybe we should rest here for a while." Erin could see that her two companions were ready for a break.

Katelyn gave a sigh of relief as she twirled the backpack off her shoulder. She was the youngest of the three at age 27. Her strength was a surprising feature given her small stature. A smooth quartz boulder accommodated the three as a surprisingly comfortable lounge while affording a view of the landscape. Erin Roberts felt more at home here than in her hometown of Ontario. She had accompanied her father on several of his fishing excursions to this area throughout the past three decades. She had apparently inherited her father's rugged outdoor ways. Now at 36, she was still in excellent condition to meet the demands of this trail that had earned a high difficulty rating. She was surprised that her two companions were doing as well as they were in keeping up with her pace. Preparation had paid off. They still had at least a six-day journey ahead of them.

Katelyn turned to Tamara. "How would you relate this to the scenery in Haiti?" she asked.

"That's like trying to compare two beautiful babies. Each is beautiful in its own special, God-given way. But you can be sure of this. Haiti is so very beautiful. Like this lake below, the water is crystal clear, teeming with life. The jungle is lush, also filled with wondrous plant and animal life. It is truly paradise."

"Then why did your father take your family away from that paradise?" Katelyn was curious.

Erin chimed in. "Paradise lost perhaps."

"It was not an easy decision. My father had a good job as a deep-sea fishing guide. We were better off than most. We were content with what we had. But my father was concerned about the welfare of my two sisters and me. Almost two-thirds of the men in Haiti did not have a job. Women were expected to marry, have babies, and that is it. The leadership had become corrupt. In 2021, our president was assassinated, and the entire population erupted in chaos and . . . how do you say . . . destriksyon?"

"Destruction?" Erin offered.

"Well, kind of so, yes. You know . . . disorder. Mayhem?"

"Yes, mayhem. I see," Katelyn replied.

"Our fathers knew each other," Erin interjected. "My family had taken a holiday in Haiti in 2017. My father wanted to do some deep-sea fishing, so he was directed to Tamara's father's boat. Tamara and I were the same age and became close friends. We have stayed in touch since that time."

Tamara continued. "Then when my father made the difficult decision to take us out of Haiti, he contacted his very good friend in Canada who helped him get a job as a fishing guide. Several years later, we all became Canadian citizens."

"Did you consider joining the Haitian community in Quebec?" Katelyn asked.

"No. Not really. We knew Erin's family, and they offered us help. We spoke English as well as Creole. This became our home."

"That's fascinating, Tamara." Katelyn then paused briefly. "How do you like it here?" she asked. "I mean especially considering the vast differences in climate."

Tamara turned to face her two friends. She laughed. "Yes, it took some time to adjust to the snow and ice. I never even saw snowfall until I came to Canada. But please understand. I am very grateful to be here. I have learned to be content wherever God places me. When in Haiti, I was content. Most people in Haiti are content even though they are very poor. I have found that it is not quite this way for Canadians and Americans. You are always striving for more and more."

"Well, yes, I suppose that's true." Katelyn turned to Erin who nodded in agreement. "But isn't that a good thing?"

"I will say this. In Haiti, although people are content, they lack ambition."

"Why is that?" Katelyn asked.

"As I said, there is much corruption and very little chance for advancement. Let me tell you. My family belonged to a loving church in Haiti. Money, clothing, and food were given to the church regularly by some churches in America. This was a good thing, but it caused my dear brothers and sisters to stop trying to better themselves. That is how I saw it anyway. I love my Haiti, and I love my old friends, but Haitians could learn some things from you Canadians. Yes, you strive to succeed. Thankfully my father was not typical. He knew that God had brought us to this land. He knew he must work hard, and he did so."

"So you think *God* brought you here?" Erin's statement held an element of derision.

"Oh yes. 'The mind of a person plans his way, but the Lord directs his steps.' That comes from Proverbs 16 verse 9. God has been my guide all of my life."

"You're always quoting Bible verses, Tamara. It gets kind of old sometimes," Erin scoffed.

"Leave her alone. She can believe whatever she wishes," Katelyn replied. "Tamara has her truth. You have yours."

"Oh no, no, no!" Tamara interrupted as she stood up. Tamara's bold manner had a way of gaining immediate attention.

Erin looked at Katelyn as if to say, "You have no idea the can of worms you just unleashed."

"My dear friends. Do you not see this?" Tamara stretched out her arms. "Do you see that mountain range? Do you see those beautiful lakes below? What did we see last night under the canopy of the night sky? Was it not Le Lait Fason?"

"The what?" interrupted Erin.

"The Milky Way." Tamara corrected herself. "And we have all seen the astonishing northern lights."

Erin was accustomed to hearing Tamara's oratory sermons. She gave Katelyn a smile of amused tolerance.

Tamara continued. "Do you not see the hand of God? It is beautiful, is it not? It sings to us a love song. It is poetry. God's poetry. It tells me something. I see the One who is far above my own small self. I will not dare to judge this One and say to Him that He is not real or powerful or that He is insignificant."

"Tamara, we really need to . . ." Erin tried to interject.

"I am not finished." Tamara took another breath and continued in her usual vigorous way. "So now . . ." she reached into a side pocket of her backpack. "Do you see this?" She pulled out a Creole Bible. "This book tells me about this One who speaks to us through His poetic love song of creation. Now I can know Him. This book speaks *His* truth. Not my truth. Not someone else's truth. Do you see?"

"Are you finished now?" Erin teased. "We need to get back on the trail and set up camp by mid-afternoon."

"Yes, yes, I am finished . . . for now," she chuckled. Erin and Katelyn joined her in laughter, knowing there was more in store.

CHAPTER 14

MAY 26, 2028
DAY 6 ON THE SILHOUETTE TRAIL KILLARNEY
PROVINCIAL PARK IN ONTARIO, CANADA

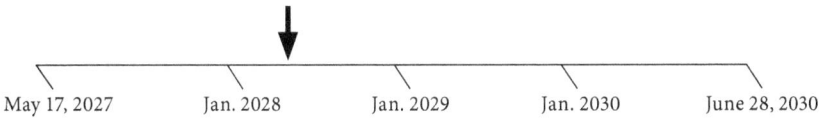

| May 17, 2027 | Jan. 2028 | Jan. 2029 | Jan. 2030 | June 28, 2030 |

The morning of day six along the Silhouette Trail was greeted with drizzle and fog covering Boundary Lake where the three had set up camp the night before. A climb up Silver Peak, the highest point in the park, was their objective for the day. After reaching the summit, they descended back to the main trail and arrived at Silver Lake to set up camp in the late afternoon. All three had managed to get blisters and were now finding relief in the chilly waters of Boundary Lake. Katelyn had prepared biscuits on a Coleman stove. She filled the biscuits with honey, dried fruit, and nuts, and topped them off with cinnamon and sugar.

"These are delicious," Erin remarked.

"Thanks."

"Delightful," Tamara added. "But these blisters are not. They are killing me."

Erin chimed in. "As my father used to always say, 'Keep your socks and your biscuit mix dry.' Well, at least the mix is dry." Erin began drying off her feet as she reached for dry socks.

"Erin, how long will it take us to get to the top of Silver Peak?" Katelyn asked.

"All right, let's talk about our itinerary. It should take us three to four hours to reach the peak, but that is on a dry path. We may encounter several marshy spots as well as slick granite, so it might take a bit longer. We all need to take extra precautions with our footing. Then once we reach the top, we are going to want to rest and take in the view. Hopefully, the fog will lift. It will take us a little more than an hour to get back down to the main path and then another hour and a half to get to Silver Lake to set up camp."

"Sounds like a pretty tight schedule. And that doesn't even include rest stops or lunch," Katelyn added.

"Right. So, ladies, we'd better break camp and be on our way."

"Oh lordy, my poor feet." Tamara was slow in removing her feet from the cool water. Erin took out her first aid kit and helped Tamara apply moleskin to the tender portions of her feet.

"Remember to keep dry socks handy just in case."

"I will. Thank you, dear friend."

It took a bit longer to break camp due to the mist that had covered the tent fabric. They needed to dry the surface with some chamois they carried for that purpose. Erin tried to find the forecast for the area on her phone but was unable to get good reception. She would have to wait until they reached higher elevation. The fog was lifting as they got underway around 10:30 a.m. Their first hour's trek took them along a gradual increase in elevation. Although the fog was not as intense, a mist still hung in the air. The morning had been quite chilly when they first set off, which was somewhat of a relief from the warmer days behind them. They passed and exchanged greetings with several other hikers moving in a counterclockwise direction along the Silhouette Trail. The trees stood tall and majestic along the path. A woodpecker's hammering was heard high above. Other birds serenaded them with a chorus of song. Colorful mushrooms dotted the path. They saw fields of purple and yellow daisies through breaches in the forest.

"My friends, do you see these beautiful flowers?" Tamara pointed to a blanket of daisies in a nearby field.

Erin sighed. "Tamara, you are always asking us if we see things. Yes, we see them. And yes, they are quite stunning."

Katelyn poked Erin with her walking stick and then turned to Tamara. "So Tamara, what were you going to say?" she asked.

"Jesus once pointed to the flowers in the field and said that even Solomon . . . do you two know who he was?" They shrugged their shoulders as they kept stride. "He was a wealthy king over Israel long before Jesus walked the Earth. Anyway, Jesus said that even Solomon was not as well dressed as these flowers. Then he added that God cares for His children even more than He cares for those flowers. And there is not a bird that falls to the ground without God knowing about it, and we are of much more value than they."

"Oh really? Does God care for all of those starving children in Africa?" Erin chided Tamara.

"Yes, He does, Erin. It is hard for us to understand and see that, I know. But God is love, my friend. And He is in control even when it appears He is not."

Erin was about to respond when Katelyn once again poked her with her walking stick.

"If you say so, Tamara." Erin seemed to quicken her pace as she spoke.

"Erin, God loves you. But you resist Him. God showed you His love by sending His Son, Jesus, to die for our sins. We must realize our tendency to push God away. Our hearts are far from God. He is waiting for us all to receive His Son, to receive His forgiveness and new life—and His love. We must not resist Him, dear sisters."

Katelyn remained silent. She did not want to contribute to any mounting tension. A heavy silence hung in the air, interrupted only by heavy breathing. Finally, Tamara spoke up.

"I am sorry, Erin. I know I come across as a stern judge and uncaring. Please forgive me."

"Can't you just enjoy the beauty of this area without bringing God into it?"

Tamara chose to remain silent.

Katelyn looked at her watch. "If I'm not mistaken, we are about 30 minutes away from the base of Silver Peak. Do you want to stop for a lunch break soon?

"Let's give it another 20 minutes," Erin suggested. They both nodded in agreement.

A welcome descent comprised the next several minutes. All three knew the path would begin to ascend before long, so they prepared their minds for the climb. Lunch consisted of an orange and a protein bar. They usually reserved dinnertime for a more exotic meal of dehydrated meat and vegetables.

Erin was now able to check her phone for a more precise weather forecast. Katelyn spoke up. "So what's the verdict?"

"It's really hard to say. The weather here is very unpredictable, but it appears we'll escape those storm clouds we see off to the northwest. I say we keep to our agenda and climb that mountain." The others reluctantly agreed. Tamara took off her shoes to examine her sores and give her feet some relief.

"How are your blisters doing, Tamara?" Erin asked.

"Surprisingly well," replied Tamara as she slipped her socks and shoes back on. "I think I'm okay to keep going."

"Yeah, we gotta get a move on," declared Erin as she prepared to move out.

Katelyn broke out in song. "Gotta get a move on. Don't make me wait, girl. Gotta get a move on. Don't make us late, girl."

"Hey, I know that song!" Shouted Tamara as she continued the next line. "Together we have a destination. So let there be no hesitation."

"Do you know this song, Erin?" asked Katelyn.

"You better believe I do. 'Yeah, baby, gotta get a move on, the ends in sight girl. Gotta get a move on, follow the light, girl.'"

All three began to sing in three-part harmony as they moved in unison sway. "Yeah, together we'll follow that light. So gotta get a move on. Gotta get a move on."

All three kept the melody going for another minute or so as they trudged ahead, eventually closing in an explosion of applause and laughter.

"Oh my, oh my." Tamara could hardly contain her laughter. "We should form a group and perform in Haiti. I tell you. We would become famous there." They were all in wholehearted agreement.

They were met by a small group of hikers coming down from the peak. They exchanged knowing smiles, everyone amused by the chorus that had most definitely been heard by all a few seconds before. After the downhill hikers passed, the three women exploded once again in laughter.

It took several minutes before the three were able to contain themselves and set off on their uphill climb. And climb they did. The climb was hazardous. Trees still lined the periphery of the trail, surrounding the large, smooth outcroppings of granite that were wet from the mist. They maneuvered past several loose boulders as Erin led the way. She paused. The others welcomed the momentary breather.

"Ladies, my pack is becoming quite heavy." The others nodded in agreement. "And I'm afraid it is going to knock us off balance. I suggest we leave them here near that final row of tall pines. We'll climb to the peak and then pick them up on the way back down."

"Are you sure they'll be safe here?" Katelyn asked.

"Oh, yes. Everyone here is a kindred spirit. We all support one another. No one will disturb our packs."

"Then I say good plan," Katelyn added.

"My feet are in perfect agreement." Tamara took a deep breath and let it out slowly. "Are you ready, feet?" She looked down, expecting her feet to respond. "They shall climb and not grow weary," she muttered to herself.

"What was that, Tamara?" Katelyn asked.

"Oh, nothing. My feet are happy and ready to climb."

The three left their packs about a third of the way up the mountain. They made a mental note of the location and set off. The ascent was taking them much longer than anticipated. The rocks were wet and unstable, causing them to lose their footing from time to time. Up to this point, no ankles had succumbed to a sprain or strain. The anticipated view from the top kept them going. Their ambition paid off as they reached the summit.

Tamara began to cry tears of joy. "I have never seen such a beautiful sight in all my life," she uttered through her tears.

"Didn't I tell you?" Erin was smiling as she leaned over to rest her hands on her knees.

"This has made all the pain and effort worthwhile." Katelyn found a rock to sit on. She lay back in a supine position. All three took a brief moment of rest. Out came the phones as each snapped away at the scenic beauty, being sure to include themselves in the photos to add credence to their adventures in the wild.

Erin looked again at the forecast and weather map on her phone. "Oh, dear me," she said. "The storm is headed this way. We'd better start back down right away."

By now the time was a little past 3:00 p.m. Erin bent down to touch her toes and then stood erect. The others followed suit. It was going to be slow going. Within minutes the air was filled with sprinkles. They cautiously quickened their pace. By 3:30, the rain began to pour. The wind, too, had begun to whip up. Fortunately, each hiker had remembered to bring along a rain jacket. Here they were, exposed on top of slick granite, trying to maneuver their way past loose stones. They saw the sky light up over what appeared to be Three Narrows Lake. They counted. Thirty seconds went by. It was perhaps six miles away. But a second strike hit even closer within seconds of the first. Then a third. The sound of thunder rolled throughout the canyon.

"What should we do, Erin?" Katelyn's voice held an element of panic.

"Just keep going. Once we reach our packs, we'll set up a makeshift camp. We will need to get the tent up quickly."

The three made good time despite the hazards along the route. They did not see any other hikers. Erin felt foolish for insisting they keep going up the mountain. "I'm so sorry, ladies." Tamara and Katelyn both reassured Erin that she was not to blame for this unexpected predicament.

"Over there," Katelyn announced. They quickly converged on their packs, taking out the tent and setting it up amidst the wind that was now gusting to perhaps 60 or more miles per hour. The rain pelted them as they struggled to set up the tent. It took the efforts of all three to finally get the tent staked down. They carefully attached the rain tarp and gave it extra tension to make sure it would not blow away. All three crawled inside and zipped up the front opening. By now the lighting and thunder had reached within a mile or so of their location. Each looked at the other with sighs of relief.

"Do you think we're safe here?" Katelyn asked.

"Those tall pines just to our northwest will provide a wind and rain break but are far enough away to avoid a lightning strike."

"I will pray for us now. Will you join me?" Tamara offered.

"Of course, Tamara." Erin respectfully replied. Katelyn nodded in agreement.

Tamara bowed her head and kept silent for a moment. The other two looked at one another, wondering if this was merely a silent prayer. Tamara lifted her hands, palms up.

"My gracious Father, I bless Your name. I thank You that You allow us to come boldly before Your throne because of Jesus, our Mediator, who gives us this privilege. Now, Father, I thank You that You have given us such a wonderful journey this week. We have had the privilege of seeing Your beautiful and marvelous creation in this small part of our world. We thank You for Your care for us along our journey. Now, Father, I ask that You keep us safe from harm. We know that the wind and rain and lightning can create fear in our hearts, but You tell us not to fear. You have told us to trust You no matter what happens in life. May You bring peace to our hearts as we just experience and marvel at Your power and strength. I thank You for loving us and caring for us. I pray this now in the mighty name of Jesus, my Lord. Amen."

Tamara lowered her hands. She kept her head bowed low for a moment longer as the two friends raised their heads.

Katelyn turned to Tamara. "That was a sweet gesture, Tamara."

The storm was on top of them now. The wind battered against the sides of the tent. Torrents of rain continued to beat against the tent, but it was sturdy and held back any attempt by the rain to enter their dry domain.

The time was now 5:00 p.m. Erin spoke up. "Even if the storm passes, we won't have time to make it to our next campsite. We'll stay here for the night."

Tamara hesitated to mention her current condition but realized she really had no choice. "Um, ladies, I have to go." They both knew what she meant. The other two had relieved themselves at a latrine near the top of the peak. Tamara had not. Now she was desperate. "I just can't wait. So I'll find a spot somewhere out there and be back soon."

She received an understanding nod from her two companions. She had already taken off her walking boots. Not wanting to take the time to put them back on, she chose flip-flops instead. She slipped on her rain jacket and unzipped the opening to the tent. I'll try to be quick," Tamara said as she passed through the opening.

"Be careful," Erin implored.

Tamara stepped out and was immediately pelted with horizontal wind and rain. She looked around. She spotted an area perhaps 20 yards farther down the incline. It was a miserable task under the conditions, but she was now able to relax. She began to move back toward the tent when a sudden gush of water rounded a boulder and knocked her off her feet. The granite slope was smooth but contained many loose rocks and boulders. Tamara began to slide feet first as she tried to catch herself or find something to grab hold of as the momentum carried her farther down the slope. "Oh, dear Father, help me," she cried. The rain continued to pelt her face as she continued her downward course. She felt and heard a snap as her right foot slammed into a large rock, causing it to descend just behind her. For a brief moment, she felt herself flying through the air as the face of one granite surface was replaced by another some four feet below. Upon impact, her head flew back, knocking her unconscious as she continued her downward course, now being flung against the rocks and stones, some of which were loosened and joined her on her downward flight. She came to a sudden halt as her body slammed against a large outcrop. One of the boulders that had come loose was tumbling straight for the now-unconscious victim. Narrowly missing her head, it smashed against her right foot that was already wedged against the outcropping. Tamara let out a screech. The others were unable to hear her cry through the thunderous roar in the canyon.

Minutes passed before Katelyn finally inquired about Tamara's whereabouts. "Shouldn't Tamara be back by now?" she asked.

"Right. I'll go check on her." Erin slipped on her rain jacket and stepped out of the tent. "Tamara?" she yelled. No answer came. She stepped out farther. "Tamara?" she called louder. Still no answer. By this time, Katelyn had joined her outside the tent.

Thunder still rumbled throughout the canyon. The wind was strong, but the rain had turned to a light horizontal sprinkle. Katelyn joined Erin in calling out to Tamara. "Oh, no. Something's happened. We need to find her," Katelyn declared.

"Look down there." Erin spotted something farther down the granite surface. They cautiously moved down the sloping surface. "It's one of Tamara's flip-flops."

Both women then heard a faint voice in the distance. "Tamara, is that you?" Erin shouted.

"Help me!" came a faint voice.

"Tamara, keep talking," Erin screamed.

The two women were stunned to see where Tamara had landed. A distance of some 100 yards was between Tamara and the tent. Upon approaching her, Katelyn had to stop and turn away. She immediately saw her condition and the snare that kept her pinned against the outcropping. She turned to Erin and whispered, "Erin, she is in serious condition. We can't move her. I'm not sure we can unlodge her from that boulder."

"We don't know that yet," Erin urged. They moved forward.

"Tamara, we're here. Let's check you out."

"Oh, dear friends, what a mess I've made." Tamara tried to add a touch of humor to her words, but she was experiencing great pain. Her voice was weak due to what felt like broken or bruised ribs.

The two friends dared not move or turn Tamara over until they checked her thoroughly for any signs of broken bones or major gashes. "My right side and foot hurt most," she muttered. Tamara mentioned losing consciousness for a brief moment in the fall. Erin studied Tamara's eyes for any sign of head injury.

Erin turned to Katelyn. "Move farther up the hill, and try to call the emergency number from that photo we took of the sign at the park office. I'll stay here."

Erin had failed to bring her first aid kit with her when she stepped out of the tent. Tamara's ribs were bruised but seemed to be intact. She could not be certain. Erin asked Tamara more questions to ensure there was no concussion. She was in surprisingly good shape from having slid so far down the granite structures. But her lower right leg and foot were another matter.

"Tamara, talk to me. How are you doing?"

Tamara strained to speak. "Dear friend. My foot aches so. Can you see it?"

Erin hesitated to describe what she was seeing. Not only was Tamara's foot pinned between an outcrop and a boulder, but it was twisted in an unnatural state. "Well, Tamara, it appears you are trapped between a rock and a hard place." Tamara tried to laugh but found it difficult due to her painful right side. "Katelyn is calling for help. We'll get you out of here."

Katelyn came back down to join them. "I'm not getting any service at all."

Erin raised her voice. "Didn't you try moving around? Come on, Katelyn, you have to keep trying. We can't leave Tamara here."

Both Erin and Katelyn were on edge. Erin, who usually held her composure, was now beginning to panic. Katelyn was unsure of what to do. Tamara could sense their tension. She wanted to reassure her friends. Through labored breathing, she uttered, "Ladies, God will see me through this. He will see us all through this ordeal. Yes, it hurts, but He knows. Something will work out. You will see."

Erin was exasperated by Tamara's apparent naivety. "Tamara, I need to be upfront with you. If we don't get help soon . . . well . . . you may lose your foot or worse. And who knows what else might be wrong. I heard your prayer, you know. You prayed for God's care. And He allowed this? This is how He answered your prayer?" Erin knew immediately she should not have used such harsh words with her friend. Her anger was beginning to surface.

"I do not know why this happened other than my own foolish ways. Even still, God is in control."

Lightning lit up the sky just to their south. Wind gusts came and went. Thunder continued to rumble through the valley below. They heard a cracking sound and a loud crash intermixed with the roll of thunder. Erin looked up. "What was that?"

"I'm not sure." Katelyn was perplexed.

"Katelyn, get back up there and try again. Please. We have to find help." Katelyn sighed and then headed back up the mountain to a higher elevation.

Erin was now in tears as she stroked the head of Tamara who was now beginning to moan in pain. "Tamara, why did God let this happen to you? You love Him, and this is how He repays that love?"

"I do not know why, my friend. I must trust Him in the good times and the bad. He always supplies me with everything I need. 'And my God will supply all your needs according to His riches in glory in Christ Jesus' (Phil. 4:19). He has spoken these words to me in His book."

"Good Lord, Tamara, what does that mean? Come back to reality, girl. This is bad. Really bad. I just don't get how you can continue to be so pious. Get real. You're stuck here on this mountain. No one is here to help us. Don't you get that?"

"Peace, my friend."

Katelyn suddenly appeared accompanied by two other hikers. "I found help and . . ." One of the two interrupted her.

"I'm Franco. This is Sean. We heard you when you were shouting for your friend and headed this way. Katelyn found us. We're here to help."

Erin stood and peered at the two men as if they were angels. Franco was around six foot four and must have weighed over 300 pounds. The other was much shorter but just as stout. "We're firefighters," Sean said. Erin was suddenly conscious of her own open mouth and closed it.

"I'm Erin, and this unfortunate friend is Tamara."

Tamara raised her hand. "Thank you, Jesus."

Erin turned to look at Tamara in amazement. Tamara just smiled. "Did I not say, my friend?"

Sean began checking Tamara over and carefully bandaged her wounds. Franco then said, "The first thing we must do is move this stone, but we'll need to pry it loose without putting more pressure on Tamara's foot." Franco knew the boulder was too large and bulky to move by strength alone. The two men were unable to position themselves over the boulder in such a way that it could be dislodged. Franco motioned to Sean to find a large, thick branch for leverage. Sean found a freshly fallen tree. He checked it for strength and integrity. Franco found another large stone to use as a fulcrum. They carefully placed the stone near the boulder. With the use of their knives, they dug a ditch under the stone that had trapped Tamara's foot. This is where they would place the end of the lever. The idea was to allow the boulder to dislodge without rolling across Tamara's foot or ankle any more than it already had. It would then roll away down the incline.

"Are you ready, Tamara?" Sean asked.

She gave a reassuring nod. Franco then began to place his full weight on the lever. Sean positioned himself over the boulder, making sure it would move in the intended direction. Sure enough, the branch took the strain, and the boulder began to move. Franco and Sean strained further to wedge it free of Tamara's foot. Sean had a good grasp on the boulder. "A little bit more, Franco." Tamara let out a yelp as the boulder slid off her foot. Erin looked down at Tamara's foot and grimaced. What was attached to the end of Tamara's leg was no longer recognizable as a foot.

"*She will lose it for sure*," she whispered to herself. Erin tried to keep her composure but had to look away.

Franco took out a sock from his backpack and then dipped it in a pool of cold rainwater. "Here, Sean, to keep the swelling down." Sean first wrapped the foot in gauze and then laid the wet sock over the top of Tamara's foot. He then added another layer of ace bandage. "Franco and I will fix up a stretcher from our jackets and walking poles." He handed Katelyn his phone. "Here, this phone will give you the reception you need. Go back up to where we first met. In my phone is a direct line to the Sudbury Air Ambulance Service. Tell them we will meet them just north of the intersection of the main path and the Silver Peak path. There is an open area there. They will know the spot." Katelyn and Erin knew the location.

"And don't worry. We will be careful with your friend. Oh, and tell them that Franco and Sean told you to call. They know us. We should arrive about the same time they do. I would suggest you two go back to your base camp to gather your gear and then meet us at the spot. Just be sure you hurry back. Otherwise, we will have to leave you," Sean added. "Besides, I would like to have my phone back." He smiled as they continued constructing the stretcher.

Tamara began to whimper in pain as her foot started to swell. "Before we depart, I would like to offer up a prayer," she spoke through labored breathing.

"Please, Tamara. No more prayers right now. We need to get you to safety," Erin pleaded.

"No. We must pray." Tamara's stern words were enough to cause everyone to immediately halt in obedient compliance as she began to voice her petition.

"Dear Father. You see what is happening to all of us here. You know our hearts." Tamara's voice was even weaker than before, but no one dared to interrupt. "You know our needs. Not just my needs, Father. We all are in need of You, dear Father. I thank You, dear Father, for sending me these two strong men to help me. And I thank You for my two dearest friends here who came to my rescue. They, too, need reassurance and help to make it through this ordeal. Watch over them tonight, and give them peace as You have given me peace. It is in my precious Jesus's name I pray, Amen." Tamara then added, "I will see you two shortly. My two angels here will see to that."

As the two men completed the makeshift stretcher, Erin and Katelyn started back up the mountain to their campsite. Katelyn did as Sean had directed and successfully reached the Sudbury Air Ambulance rescue team. She relayed their condition and intended position. They said it would take them about 30 minutes to arrive. That would give them all plenty of time to reach the rendezvous point.

"Now let's get to our tent. We need to . . ." Erin was unable to complete her sentence.

Katelyn turned to Erin. "That's what I wanted to tell you before. We don't have a base camp. When I came back up to try again to call for help, I . . ."

"What do you mean? Our tent, Katelyn. We need to get back to our tent."

Katelyn took Erin by the hand and led her up the distance to the location of their tent. There before them lay the crumpled heap of what was once their tent and supplies. A large pine tree had dislodged in the high wind and now lay directly on top of where the three had waited out the storm. "That was the crashing sound we heard earlier. If Tamara had not left and we had not gone looking for her, we all three would have been crushed." Katelyn left Erin to her thoughts as they both pondered the scene before them.

Erin's thoughts raced. Dozens of unanswered questions flooded her mind. Tamara's remarks about God, her prayers, her strength, her peace and trust, her faith . . . yes, Tamara's faith in her God. Erin began to cry uncontrollably. She was, first of all, angry that God allowed all of this to happen. She could not understand. She remembered that Tamara did not trust her own ability to control her surroundings. Tamara simply placed her trust in this One she perceived as having control over her life. "Control?" Erin thought. "If He were truly in control, then why did He allow any of this to happen?" Erin then thought of the sacrifice of

Tamara's foot that made it possible for them all to live. The fallen tree may have killed them all. *"So why would God even allow the tree to fall?"* she wondered. Erin's anger turned to a resigned acceptance of the reality of the situation. Whether she understood or not, she saw that everything that had taken place not only rescued them from a terrible death but had prompted this newfound revelation within her soul. It would take some time for Erin to grasp the impact of this night. Meanwhile, a sense of guilt began to rise in Erin's heart. "It's my fault," she whispered to herself and then repeated aloud, "This is my fault."

Erin felt Katelyn's embrace as they both continued to sob. The air was still filled with mist from the rain. It mixed with their tears as they both looked to heaven and felt a calm assurance come over their spirits.

"Erin, we need to leave. We won't be able to retrieve anything. It's gone, Erin. We need to go."

Erin exhaled slowly as if to regain her strength and tenacity to keep persevering. Arm in arm, Katelyn and Erin started down the mountain.

CHAPTER 15

JUNE 10, 2028
ERIN ROBERTS' DRIVE TO THE HOME OF TAMARA TOUSSAINT OTTAWA, ONTARIO

May 17, 2027	Jan. 2028	Jan. 2029	Jan. 2030	June 28, 2030

Erin Roberts reached over to turn off the car radio. Music usually helped calm her spirit, but she was too deep in thought, and the music was a distraction. It had now been a little over two weeks since the incident on the Silhouette Trail. Erin still struggled with painful thoughts about Tamara's terrible accident. *"I saw her foot and ankle,"* she thought. Erin tried to put the dreadful image out of her mind, but it still continued to haunt her thoughts. "It's all my fault," Erin kept telling herself, and she was too ashamed to give her devoted friend a call. She did eventually try to call Tamara during her stay in the hospital, but there was no answer. Erin was relieved by the failed call. She didn't know what to say to her friend whose life had changed so abruptly as she faced an uncertain future. The plaguing thoughts were now causing her to perform poorly on the job. On top of that, the Thought Transmission team called her to come in for her first experiment. She knew she had to comply or would have been taken off the team. The session that day had not given them the results they expected. Once back home, she decided to call Katelyn. Perhaps she could provide comfort. Katelyn tried to reassure Erin that she had no reason to feel guilt. After all, it was the storm that was to blame. Katelyn brought up the fact that things could have been much worse. They both did what they could that day, and Tamara was rescued despite their worst fears. Katelyn mentioned to Erin that she had spoken with Tamara. They had a pleasant chat.

Over the past week, Tamara sensed Erin was feeling a sense of shame. She ended up calling her dear friend Erin after coming through her initial surgery. Tamara would be home soon and invited Erin to come and visit. The call brought some level of relief to Erin. "Why is Tamara so upbeat?" Erin wondered, but she realized it was typical of this woman who had already faced several trials in her life with the same attitude of settled peace. The call allowed Erin to muster the courage to visit her friend. Now, today, she was heading across town to see her dear companion for the first time since the accident. As she drove, a smile finally arose on her face. She was becoming excited about connecting once more with Tamara.

A knock on the door was followed by "Come in, dear friend." Erin opened the door and walked into the living room where she found Tamara sitting in an easy chair with her leg elevated on an ottoman. Tamara's bandaged foot seized Erin's entire attention for the moment. She looked at Tamara's smiling face and then back at the foot before finally speaking.

"Oh, Tamara," was all Erin could muster as she immediately began to weep. Here she was hoping to be a comfort and support for her friend but instead was now having to be consoled by this woman of strength and courage. "It is fine, my friend." Tamara, too, began to weep. "It is fine," she repeated. Erin walked up and bent over, wrapping her arms around her friend's neck. "Oh, Tamara, I am so sorry."

They both continued to weep. Finally, Tamara's mood turned from tears to laughter. She knew Erin usually wore a cap with hair bound up in a ponytail but now observed Erin with an apparent pixie cut up under her cap. "Oh my, look at your hair. You cut it so short." Tamara had never seen Erin with such a radical change in hairstyle.

Erin ignored Tamara's observation. She was still troubled by her friend's painful struggles as well as her own contribution to this terrible tragedy in Tamara's life.

"Tamara, I . . ." Erin was interrupted by Tamara's gentle voice.

"My dear friend, please know none of this has anything to do with you. Katelyn told me that you were feeling shame. There is no need for that. At what point do we stop blaming ourselves for mishaps and simply accept that these things happen?"

Erin had always been amazed at Tamara's insight and her ability to voice such wisdom. Erin usually resisted many of the words Tamara expressed, especially concerning God and Jesus. She was still a bit uncomfortable when the conversation veered in that direction. But she was here as a support for her friend, not a judge.

"Then why am I still so troubled?" Erin could not shake the guilt and shame she felt in her heart.

Tamara paused for a moment and then gave Erin a reassuring smile. "Perhaps you are allowing your troubled thoughts to control your mind rather than speaking to yourself what is really true."

"What on earth are you talking about, Tamara?"

"You see, my friend, we all have a choice." Tamara wasn't sure just how to adequately explain her words. Then she recalled a short psalm she had read recently. "I am reminded of a psalm of David."

Erin looked up but thought to herself, "*Oh, here we go. She is going to bring up Jesus again.*"

Tamara continued. "You see, King David of Israel loved God and trusted God but still faced problems and persecution from many people and places. He wrote many psalms where he pleaded to God for help. Let me tell you about one of these. It is very short, only five verses. It is Psalm 43, I think." Tamara reached for her Bible on the table beside her chair. She turned to the 43rd Psalm. "Yes, Psalm 43. It begins like this. David cried out to God for help against his enemies. He was so very troubled, you see. He was listening to his troubled mind and becoming more and more upset."

"Like me," Erin suggested.

"Yes, and me too."

This admission surprised Erin. "You?"

"Yes. I have had many anxious thoughts about what has happened. I, too, have wondered how this could happen to me. I told my God, "I trusted you to keep me from harm." But then He allowed all of this. I began to think of other times when troubles came my way or have come to my family and friends, especially those I left behind in Haiti. I even began to question God's goodness. But let me tell you something. I hope that what I say will bring you comfort as I, too, have been comforted."

"Okay. I'm listening." Erin usually resisted such a speech from Tamara. But Tamara had aroused her curiosity. She wanted to hear more.

"After David complained to his God, he then reminded God that he had always trusted in His protection. David was sure that God must have rejected him now. Yes, this God in whom he had always placed his trust must surely have turned His back on him. But then something began to happen inside David's heart. David began to speak the truth to himself rather than listen to the turmoil in his soul. He knew the truth about God, so he reminded himself that God was full of light and truth. He asked his God of truth and light to lead him through these miserable times and back into God's eternal home. By verse 4 of this psalm, David made a choice. He began to think about God's words of truth and upon His mercy. David stopped listening to his tormented soul and began to focus on God's eternal words of truth. David said he will go to the altar of God where he will find much joy. He made the choice that I said we must all make. We must all choose to trust in God's care. God's goodness, you see. David began to praise God. He asked himself, 'Why am I in such distress?'"

Up to this point, Tamara had used her own words to tell of David's spiritual journey. She then looked down at her Bible. "I want to read exactly what David says here. His final words in this psalm say this: 'Wait for God, for I will again praise Him, for the help of His presence, my God'" (Ps. 43:5). Tamara closed the Bible and placed it on her lap. Erin had been looking down but now looked up at Tamara's broad smile. "You see, dear friend, we all face many troubles in life. We can choose to either listen to our tormented thoughts or speak God's eternal truth into our minds."

"But whose truth do we listen to? Tamara, there are so many different religions around the world. What makes you think yours is true? Does that mean theirs is not? I just don't get it."

"Erin, there is an answer to your very honest question. Would you allow me to give it to you?"

"Does it involve Jesus?"

"Oh yes, dear friend. It is all about this One, this Son who claimed to be one with his Father."

"That sounds absolutely absurd." Erin tried to refrain from becoming upset. She knew that perhaps Tamara had an explanation. She would give her the respect she knew she deserved.

Tamara continued. "I know. This sounds foolish until you receive what I am about to tell you. Shall I go on?"

"Sure, go ahead. I promise to listen with an open mind."

"All right, then." Tamara paused briefly and prayed silently for the Lord's direction before speaking. "Jesus once asked His followers, 'Who do people say I am?' They told Him what they had heard from the people. Even today many people try to grasp who this Jesus is. Do they not?" Erin thought perhaps she was supposed to answer. She shrugged. Tamara continued. "Then Jesus asked them, 'But who do you say that I am?'

One man, Peter, spoke up. 'You are the Holy One. You are the Messiah who all of Israel has been searching for since the days of the prophets who told of your coming.'

Tamara went on. "You see, Peter recognized Jesus as the Messiah who all of Israel had been looking for since the days when the prophets told of His coming. Israel was looking for this One who would deliver them from the control of their enemies. But Jesus had come for a mission much greater than this. Yes, much greater. No other man, no other holy man or religion could do what Jesus did for His people. You see, they had a far worse problem than being controlled by enemies, just as you and I and all of mankind have a much greater problem than the trials we face throughout our lives. The words foretold by the prophets of old had a name for this problem we all face. The words are also for anyone who will listen. Here is the problem we all face. Are you listening, Erin?"

"Yes, Tamara, I'm listening. Go ahead."

"Here is the problem we face. We have rejected the very One who created us. He is perfect and holy, but all of us are not. We are all born with a defiant nature. The Bible calls it sin. We are all born and then grow up saying, 'I want to live by my own set of rules.' Do we not?"

Erin interrupted. "Are you saying that we have to live by God's rules? What rules? The Ten Commandments? Nobody does that."

"That is true, Erin. No one obeys those commandments. We have all disobeyed God's law, His perfect way."

"But I have always tried to live a good life, Tamara. I'm not a bad person, even though I realize I mess up from time to time. Have I not treated you and others in the right way?"

"Erin, you are saying that you are living life by your own standards, not God's. I will not sit here and tell you that you are a bad person. But we must look at God. He is perfect and true and holy, dear friend. He is so holy that He cannot have a relationship with anyone who is not holy."

"But again, Tamara, no one is holy. Don't you get that?"

"I once again must agree with you. And that is why Jesus came to this world. God sent His Son. He did not send an angel or someone from the heavens that appeared suddenly on Earth. This Son Jesus was born a man. But He was born from the Spirit of the Almighty God as well. And yes, I know that sounds like a far-reaching thing for us to grasp. You see, all of us are sinners who try to live life according to our own ways. We decide for ourselves what is right and what is wrong as we continue to reject this holy God. And so what do we do? We make up a religion and create a god to our liking. This still does not solve our biggest problem. We are still rebellious sinners. We are unable to have a relationship with God because we do not want Him in our lives. Now consider this Jesus you hear me speak of so often. He lived a perfect life. He never strayed from His Father. His coming was spoken of everywhere in the Bible, even in the Old Testament long ago before He was born. Think of the kinds of words and songs we sing at Christmas—' Oh come, oh come Emmanuel . . . and ransom captive Israel.' Emmanuel means 'God with us.' God came to us in the form of a man in order to represent us all before this holy God."

"What do you mean 'to represent us before God'?"

"He is called 'the second Adam.' You see, the first man, Adam, because he disobeyed God in the garden, brought sin into the hearts of all his children down through all of time. He brought death to us all. But this wonderful 'second Adam,' Jesus, brings new life. He lived the perfect life, which, as you pointed out, no one has ever been able to do. But then He came, not just to give us good advice but to die on a cross for our sins. Sin is so terrible, my dear friend. He died to set the record straight before our holy God. We all deserve punishment before our perfect, holy God. We can never be good enough to stand before God on our own merits of goodness. This Jesus took our place to bring us before God our Father."

"I get what you are saying, but why would God punish Jesus if He was so good?

"He did this to show His love for us. But that is not the end of the story. No. Something wonderful happened after Jesus died and was put in the tomb. He came to life. Since our sin brings us death, this Jesus brings us life. He overcame even death, you see. All of this was told long ago in Scripture. He became our Savior. You've heard it said that Jesus saves. Right? We must come to Him and trust in this Son of God to bring us back to our God and to bring us new life."

"So what, Tamara? How does His death and supposed coming to life again have anything to do with me? I just can't accept this."

Tamara remained calm and composed even though what she really wanted to do was try to coerce Erin to believe. Tamara knew that no one comes to saving faith through coercion. Tamara wondered if she should be speaking more of the actual words from the Bible, those powerful, life-changing words, rather than conveying her own inadequate explanation.

"I have been sharing with you what is called the gospel, which means good news. Paul the Apostle wrote this: 'For I am not ashamed of the gospel, for it is the power of God for salvation to everyone who believes' (Rom. 1:16). You must believe that Jesus is the Son of God and then trust in His own sacrifice of Himself as punishment for your sins, which has made it possible for you to be brought back to God." Tamara opened her Bible to Romans 8:11. "This same Paul also wrote this: 'But if the Spirit of Him who raised Jesus from the dead dwells in you, He who raised Christ Jesus from the dead will also give life to your mortal bodies through His Spirit who dwells in you.' Did you hear that, my dear friend? God's very Spirit will come to live inside of you, helping you become the very person God wants you to be. He changes us from the inside out. We are never changed by trying to live a good life through our own effort. At the moment we believe, God puts us on a lifelong process of becoming more and more like His Son Jesus. We are not, after all, turned into perfectly obedient robots. God gave us things— resources—to help us along our new life journey. He gave us His people, His church, to help us on our journey of life. He gave us his Holy Word, the Bible, to see how to live according to God's truth. He gives us His Holy Spirit to live within our very hearts. He allows us to pray to Him. He hears our prayers, Erin. He heard my prayer on the trail that day. He has been working through all my pain. He allowed me to suffer for reasons I do not fully understand."

"How can you say that, Tamara? I mean, well, okay, I have to ask. What happened to your foot and ankle? I saw how smashed and torn up they were. I was so afraid they would amputate your foot. The thought of that kept me up at night. You know?"

"I have a remarkable story to tell you, my friend." Tamara had preferred to wait until her present discussion would come to a conclusion but decided the Holy Spirit was leading her to tell Erin this story.

"A story? I'm all ears." Erin was ill at ease about the current discourse coming from Tamara and was pleased to have the dialogue move in a different direction.

"Okay, then, my friend. Here goes." Tamara had to rearrange her sitting position and set her leg down for a while. She still had the Bible on her lap but set it aside. "Oh, my goodness, Erin, I never offered you a drink. I am so sorry. Would you care for some water or lemonade? I have some in the refrigerator."

"Oh, that's fine. But yes, now that you mention it, I could use some water." Erin stood up to enter the kitchen. "Can I get you anything?"

"Yes, please. A bottle of water would be welcome. No. Lemonade would be better. Just pour me a cup, please."

Erin returned from the kitchen bearing lemonade for Tamara and a bottle of water for herself. "So, go on. What's your story?"

Tamara took a swig of lemonade and then continued. "After I was flown to the hospital emergency room, the doctors and medical people removed the temporary bandages the firefighters had applied. I saw for the first time just how badly my foot and ankle were. I was scared, Erin. And I was in so much pain. They gave me something for the pain. I began to panic. Yes, dear friend, I was calling out to God to help me, but I was still so afraid. I heard them say that they would have to amputate my foot above the ankle. I tried to calm myself and convince myself that I could manage with only one foot. The thought of them cutting through my bone and flesh terrified me. You know? I knew nothing of what might be in store for me. I was so scared, Erin. Then something remarkable happened. One of the medical staff mentioned that a visiting foot surgeon was in the hospital as a consultant. He was there to give a lecture to other surgeons. They called him in. He did not show up right away, and I began to despair. Finally, they brought him into my room. They uncovered my wrappings before him. He stared for a moment at my foot. He then looked at me. He told me his name and asked my name. He then told me that as far as he could see, they might not have to amputate but could actually save my foot. Erin, he said he could save my foot. I immediately shouted out praises to God. I have to laugh now because my voice was heard all up and down the emergency wing of the hospital. Several medical people walked into the hall to see what all the commotion was about."

"Typical Tamara," Erin exclaimed.

"Well, by this time it was early in the morning. I was so very tired. I told my nurse that I wanted to sleep. She said that was fine but that a surgical team had been told to prep the operating room. They would wake me when it was time to go in. They would then give me anesthesia before operating. I fell asleep amidst a glimmer of hope." Tamara stopped briefly and took another swig of lemonade.

"Well, go on. Go on!" Erin was anxious to hear more.

"When I woke up, I had the feeling that nothing had happened. And I was right. I called for my nurse. She said that the damage was so severe that they could not operate right away. The surgeon was going to have to study the X-rays and then develop a plan to restore my foot. Another day passed. I was becoming a bit depressed but was not angry. I continued to pray that God would see me through this and that no matter what happened, I would be at peace about the outcome."

"I would have been petrified and so angry, Tamara."

"I don't want to come off sounding pious. I, too, was scared. I resisted the anger. God did bring me comfort, however. I continued to trust in His powerful hand. Anyway, they tried to keep me comfortable. From time to time the surgeon paid me a visit and examined my foot and ankle. He finally told me that they would start operating on my foot the next morning but that it would take several hours on the operating table. He also told me that I would have to come back from time to time for further procedures. I have had two more since that time."

"That's amazing, Tamara. But I have to ask: What about the money for all this? Has insurance come through for you?"

"That is another remarkable story, my friend. I later learned that the kind of procedure performed on my foot was—how did they refer to it? Oh, yes, a trial surgical procedure. A grant from a privately funded group provided funding for newly developing surgical procedures. The very purpose of this fund was to try to prevent amputations. The surgeon who operated on my foot was actually in the hospital to talk about this funding. I just happened to be at the right place at the right time. But no. This was the hand of God just as I had prayed. And it turned out that many other surgeons were there to learn of these new ways to save limbs. My surgery actually helped other medical people learn about these methods. So even though my work as an Ontario government employee provided basic insurance, it would not have been enough to pay for all of my procedures. The grant money paid for the remaining expenses."

Erin's mouth was now open as she took in all of this. She then burst out in laughter. She once again gave Tamara a huge hug as they both roared with enthusiastic laughter.

Tamara then took on a somber appearance. "What's wrong, Tamara?" Erin asked.

"I must tell you, dear friend, that I was so very blessed. I am still blessed as I continue to go through several more surgeries. My foot was saved. I also realize things will never be quite the same for me."

"Yes, but . . ." Erin was interrupted by Tamara.

"Wait, my friend." Let me say this." Tamara paused for a moment trying to find the right words to express to her friend. "While I have no doubt that my dear God came through for me, I am reminded . . ."

"Of?"

Tamara took a moment to gather her thoughts. "There are many others all over this world who undergo much more severe trials than what I have experienced. Many of them are very devoted followers of Christ. They have suffered tremendously and have even lost their lives in some cases for the cause of Christ."

"Right. So what about that, Tamara? Why has God not come through for them as He did for you? And why are there so many suffering people? Where is God? Why does He not act?"

"I cannot fully comprehend that. I have no acceptable answer."

"Well, then . . ."

"Wait, Erin. I need to say this. God in His Word never told us He would always deliver us out of our terrible tragedies. He says He will get us through them. There is a difference. Now let me say this. As you know, I come from a country that is the poorest in the Western Hemisphere. I have seen and experienced up close the terrible suffering of many in Haiti. We have been hit with many hurricanes through the years. One of the worst ones came in 2016. It killed many people and caused much destruction. We were also hit by a terrible earthquake in 2010. It killed over 200,000 Haitians. Then in 2021 came the devastating earthquake that killed over 2,200 of my people. I have seen these things up close. I, too, suffered. So why did God allow all this suffering and death? I have no answer, dear friend. But this I will tell you. Haiti is a land of spiritual darkness and confusion. But it is also a land of light. This light shines brightly in the darkness of my island land. When destruction came, I saw many of those living in darkness come to the light. They began to place their hope in Christ. My own father tells of a time when destruction hit the family. That caused him to stop and consider the way he was living and the direction of his life. He came to what I must call a saving knowledge of Jesus Christ. It had a great impact on our family. I was part of a church of many dedicated followers of Christ, many of who lost their lives or loved ones. I have seen how the believers cope, and I have seen how unbelievers cope."

"Was there a difference?" Tamara had Erin's attention.

"Oh, yes. The unbelievers had no hope. Some even ended their own lives. They were so very devastated. The believers, however, even though they had suffered equally as hard, had a joy about them. They carried on."

"Whoa, whoa, Tamara. You are telling me that those people were happy about all that suffering? That's perverse, Tamara. How could they be so happy in the middle of such tragedy?"

"No, Erin. That is not what I am saying. I said they were joyful even in the midst of suffering. Please let me explain."

"Sure. Go ahead."

"Happiness depends on enjoyable happenings. If we are having fun, then we are happy. If we are not enjoying things, we are unhappy. Do you see? Those believers, because of their hope in God, could still experience peace and joy in their hearts. They may not have been happy, but they still experienced the joy that comes only from our heavenly Father. Even amid such suffering, they still had hope and then offered that hope to others. I saw it, Erin. With my own eyes, I saw it, my dear friend.

"When things became very bad for me and my family, we still trusted in God's goodness to get us through. Many others did as well. As you know, my father was able to bring us to Canada. And do you know how? It was because of the goodness and generosity of your own father. I am truly humbled by that new life we have been given and now even this episode in my life."

Tears began to form in Erin's eyes. She still had doubts about the idea of a good God but kept her thoughts to herself. She was weary in struggling to make sense of it all. She tried to speak but found she could not find any words to respond to what Tamara had just shared.

Tamara spoke softly. "I am sorry, my friend if I have upset you. You are my very dear friend who I love so very much. I am sorry if I have made you feel uncomfortable speaking as I did."

"Well, Tamara, you have certainly given me much to think about. I appreciate your honesty. And do not think that I have not seen and heard you over the years. I see how you have lived out your beliefs. You continually amaze me with your hopeful and trusting attitude."

"Thank you, dear friend." Tamara suddenly looked up, startled by a thought. "Oh my, where are my manners? It has become so late. Some members of my church are bringing me food for tonight's meal. They will be staying for dinner as well. Will you stay and join us for dinner?"

"I would be honored."

The conversation between the two friends veered in the direction of earlier times, fun times, and times of laughter as well as tears. Tamara's friends from church arrived with more food than they could eat in one sitting. Tamara glanced over at Erin. Her countenance was much different than when she first arrived. Erin's spirit was softening. Tamara was grateful to see this change in her friend. She voiced a short, whispered prayer. "Bring her to yourself, dear Lord Jesus." Tamara looked forward to the day when she would be able to call Erin not only her friend but a dear sister in Christ.

CHAPTER 16

JUNE 11, 2030
THOUGHT TRANSMISSION SESSION CONTINUES AT THE GENEVA SCIENCE CONFERENCE

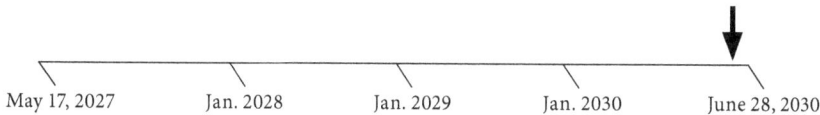

May 17, 2027   Jan. 2028   Jan. 2029   Jan. 2030   June 28, 2030

D r. Suzanne Myers continued praising and showing apprecia- tion for the team of volunteers. She then paused to regain her composure and focus. "I now want to take several minutes and take you on a journey of discovery of how we came to transmit the deepest and most intimate aspect of our being—our thoughts—from one human mind to another. Before we launch into these specifics, I want to mention a volunteer I spoke of earlier. This volunteer gave not only his brain to "the science god," as Simon Loffler put it, but also his very soul. He did not merely sit in a comfortable recliner as Simon attached probes to his skull but also brought with him an air of enthusiasm and a positive outlook to our study and to each one of our lives. There is a joy about this man that rubbed off on each of us—me especially. He and his lovely wife have both had an impact on my life. I will have him come out on stage in a few minutes, but actually, I'm not going to be the one to introduce you to him. If not for the recommendation from Nora Bernard, we would not have had the privilege of working with this man. Nora, would you come up and introduce him to us?"

Nora rose from her seat as she declared, "It would be my pleasure." She walked nervously to the microphone, holding her tablet tightly in her hand as she set it on top of the podium. Nora glanced down at the display and then back up to the audience. This was her first occasion to speak to such a large crowd. She had always heard of the fear of public speaking but had never experienced it until just now. Her voice cracked as she gave her opening statement. "It is . . . ahem . . . truly an honor to stand before you today. I have been nervous about speaking to a group of such renowned and accomplished scientists and educators as you all are." Nora became instantly aware of her childish mannerisms. She had to pause and take a breath to keep from hyperventilating before this respected crowd.

Nora looked down at her carefully constructed notes, looked up, and then continued. "Before I introduce you to this volunteer team member, I feel I need to share my heart. I must admit that I was leery of the nature of this study. It took a while before I was convinced of the legitimacy of transferring thoughts from one human mind to another. Even after I became convinced of the benefits of such an endeavor, I wondered where this technology and discovery would lead. I am sure many scientists and inventors have had to grapple with the implications of their own pursuits. But as Dr. Myers reminded me, we as scientists are about the business of discovery. That is what science does. We delve into the deepest recesses of this world and universe we live in. It is a privilege to be part of this groundbreaking project."

Nora now set her tablet containing her notes aside. "But enough of that. I am here now for another purpose. Once Dr. Myers was given the go-ahead to assemble the fine team members you met here tonight, I was given the task of recruiting volunteers. This was no easy task because each volunteer had to meet very specific requirements and attributes. I will not go into the selection criteria at this time. One candidate, in particular, had a profound influence on my life from my days in high school. I decided to take a chance that he might be a right fit and took the steps to try to contact him. I am talking about my high school science teacher, Ron Provost." Nora stepped away from the podium and motioned to the side of the stage. "Mr. Provost, come on out." As Ron walked on stage, Nora ran to give him a hug. She once again faced the audience. "Ladies and gentlemen, meet my former high school science teacher." Ron gave the audience a wave as the sound of thousands of hands coming together was amplified throughout the auditorium. Dr. Myers also walked up to the podium and spoke into the microphone. "We have asked Ron Provost to walk you through his own experience with the Thought Transmission project and then tell a little more about the journey our team has taken since the summer of 2028."

Suzanne then relinquished the microphone to Ron Provost as she and Nora walked back to their seats.

"Wow! What an amazing sight to see. I don't believe I've ever been surrounded by such an ample supply of grey matter as I see before me today." He hardly finished his sentence before the crowd responded in laughter. I want you all to know that Ms. Nora Bernard over there was certainly at the top of my list of gifted students. I am so proud to know her, and so should you."

Ron did not carry any notes. He spoke directly from his heart as he began his delivery. "I was invited by Ms. Bernard to put my name in the hat of potential volunteers. I truly had my doubts about the whole endeavor. In fact, they didn't actually fully let on about what this study was about until after I committed to it. And I must tell you, it was not an easy decision. My wife, Mona, and I discussed it and then prayed about it. But it wasn't until after I had undergone their inquest of torture . . . um, I mean, their crucible of fire." A sympathetic response erupted from the attendees. "Okay. That's what it may have felt like, but the truth is that they were actually trying to determine if I was a good match or not by giving me mind games and puzzles. That in itself is quite a story. I won't go there. So anyway, I was finally apprised of the nature of the study and asked to join the team. Once again, after much prayer and reflection, I accepted. Or, perhaps I should say that we—my wife and family— accepted the invitation."

Ron halted briefly. He glanced over at the assembled team. Dr. Suzanne Myers showed no emotion. Nora, on the other hand, broadened her smile.

"Here is my story…"

CHAPTER 17

6:12 P.M., FRIDAY, APRIL 25, 2028
INITIAL THOUGHT TRANSMISSION EXPERIMENT
ROOM B11 NEUROSCIENCE BUILDING AT
KING'S UNIVERSITY

| May 17, 2027 | Jan. 2028 | Jan. 2029 | Jan. 2030 | June 28, 2030 |

Skimming Eternity / First Thought Transmission Experiment

"Are you nervous?"

"No."

"Excited?"

"Not especially."

"Then how are you feeling?"

"Umm . . . intrigued."

"That's not a feeling, Mr. Provost," Nora declared.

"It's Ron. I'm no longer your high school teacher. We're colleagues now. Remember?"

"It just doesn't feel right to call you Ron." Nora was trying to take his mind away from the activity surrounding Ron's head. Simon Loffler, the brain scan technician, had already drawn a diagram on Ron's shaved head. Now he was placing electrodes at strategic points.

Dr. Suzanne Myers walked into the room. "Well, today's the day. Are you excited?" she asked.

"Again?" Ron thought. "Yes, very excited."

"Hey, you told me you weren't excited," Nora teased.

Ron smiled. "Always tell the boss you're excited." Nora and Suzanne chuckled. Ron then added, "But if you must know, I feel like a bull being prepared for sacrifice."

"To the science god," Simon added.

"Yep." Ron wanted to nod but remembered Simon telling him not to move his head until he had completed his work. He glanced toward Suzanne. "So, I'm curious. Is it a man or woman who is acting as the receiver?" Ron was not permitted to know the identity of the receiver.

"In this case, it's a woman," was the reply.

"And you shaved her head too?"

Suzanne raised her brow as she looked down at Ron. "Well, actually we gave her the option of either shaving all her hair or only the sections where we attach electrodes."

"Fair enough," Ron replied, and then added, "You all are really serious about this study, aren't you?" Ron had not entered into this study lightly. He and Mona had prayed about it, trusting in the Lord's guidance as they allowed the Holy Spirit to give them either a sense of peace or lack thereof. They had also considered the ethics of it all.

Nora gave her input. "Dr. Myers and I have had many discussions about whether we should even be pursuing this whole issue of passing on someone's most intimate inner secrets to another. I have had my misgivings but . . ."

Suzanne interrupted. "We've given you our reasons for taking this journey. You agreed, knowing the advantages it offers to those who struggle with neurological roadblocks. We have other motivations as well. For instance, how might this contribute to helping comatose victims or as a treatment for Alzheimer's? For all we know, it might help raise the intelligence level of some individuals. The brain is a marvelous organ. We have only begun to skim the surface of discovering its power and capability. This is science and no different than any other pursuit of science. Who knows where all of this will lead? So yes, we are really serious about this study."

Ron realized he must have touched a nerve and an area of contention between Suzanne and Nora. He decided to lighten the mood. "I can see that *you're* certainly excited."

"Absolutely." Suzanne offered an agreeable smile.

"We're good to go." Simon stood back, admiring his handiwork as if it were a sculptured work of art.

"Very good," Suzanne responded as Nora noted the time and wrote something down on her tablet. "All right, Mr. Transmitter. You know the drill. We will give you two or three minutes alone to regain your focus. While you wait, try to concentrate on that one thought consisting of a short phrase. Nora will walk back into the room and sit behind you with her tablet. You will tell her your thought, and she will write it down along with the time. You will then concentrate only on that one thought and repeat it over and over in your mind until we tell you to stop. Simon and the others will be reading the scan while following the route your thought takes through the various segments of your brain. And so you know, we will be listening to everything you say."

Ron listened intently. He knew he was chosen partially due to his ability to concentrate on one thought at a time. While other people may struggle with attention deficit disorder, he did not. He liked to say that he was simple-minded.

Suzanne continued. "At various moments in time, we will send the activity from all those electrodes on your head to our receiver who is sitting in another room down the hall. So are you ready to get started?"

"Ready."

"Good. So Nora will step out of the room for a few minutes. When she reenters, we will begin the study. Good luck, Ron."

"*Luck won't have anything to do with it,*" Ron thought.

"Here we go." An eerie silence followed Suzanne's last words.

Ron took a moment to clear his head of impeding thoughts. He had prayed for God to grant him peace through this process. Not only did he have peace about this study but he was graced with having no other matters going on in his life trying to steal that peace. He smiled, knowing the faithfulness of God.

Inside the adjacent room, several members of the team sat fixated on the activity inside Ron's brain. There was also a visual scan of the brain of the receiver, Sylvia Ramon. Dr. Milton studied signal processing and the pathway of neurons traveling to and from various segments of Ron's brain. Simon worked the equipment and was also able to direct the pathway to various parts of Sylvia's brain. Sharon Vogel took copious notes. Miranda and Nora prepared to enter their designated rooms. Miranda Gomez was to accompany Sylvia Ramon into her room. Nora would be accompanying Ron. Dr. Myers was preparing to take her own notes. She would also be making recommendations to Simon as the experiment progressed.

Dr. Randall Milton looked up from the scan. "His mind has settled, and the pathways are consistent. It's time to start," he said. Suzanne gave Nora and Miranda a nod. They exited the room.

Nora entered the room where Ron sat staring at a blank wall in a dimly lit room. She acknowledged him and then sat down. She gave Ron a few seconds to concentrate and then asked, "What is your thought?"

"Simon says," Ron replied.

Inside the test room, Simon smiled as the others chuckled. Ron's thought was traveling along a very precise neurotransmission route in his brain.

In the adjacent room, Sylvia Ramon sat with a similar array of electrodes attached to her head. She, too, had been given instructions. She was to try to clear her mind of all but one simple thought or phrase. It was to be common terminology she spoke or heard often. This was to keep her own thoughts unique and separate from any that might come from the transmitter. She was to repeat her own thought over and over in her mind. If another thought came to her that was outside the purview of familiar expressions, she was to mention it to Miranda. One minute elapsed. Sylvia said nothing. Two minutes passed.

Inside the test room, Simon was busy attempting to adjust the pathway of thoughts from Ron to Sylvia. A third monitor was used to direct the pathway to Sylvia's mind. Simon was to open the transmission line every 15 seconds, allow it to remain open for five seconds, and then close it. Simon, Dr. Milton, and Dr. Myers were intrigued to find that the pathway of electrons entering Sylvia's mind would begin similarly to Ron's pathway but then veer off suddenly before continuing the planned route. When the circuit was closed, they could easily see the activity from Sylvia's brain. "What do you think is happening, Simon?" Suzanne asked.

"I haven't got a clue. I'm making adjustments, but the electrons won't cooperate."

Suzanne turned her attention to Randall Milton. "Dr. Milton, what do you think?"

"If Simon is making the appropriate adjustments, then either the probes on Mrs. Ramon's and Mr. Provost's heads are in the wrong location, we have a loose circuit, or something is obstructing the thoughts from being transmitted."

Simon responded. "The electrodes are in the right spot. I'm sure of it. And I double-checked that all circuits are in order. I'm guessing there is something neurological inside Sylvia's brain that is not allowing her to receive Ron's thought."

"Anything?" Miranda asked Sylvia.

Sylvia was becoming a bit anxious but took deep breaths to alleviate any tension. "Every so often my mind goes blank—literally goes blank. Or at least I lose the thought I was thinking, but then it returns after a few seconds. It is a strange experience. But nothing else comes to mind." Sylvia did not admit to another sensation she experienced when her mind went blank. During those few seconds when her mind went blank, as she put it, she felt as if her mind were reaching for a memory, perhaps from her past. This elusive memory eluded her, for she regained her focus almost immediately.

After another minute, Sylvia began to wonder if she was simply not concentrating enough. She did as they had asked and thought only of one short phrase. The phrase she concentrated on was "Mary, the mother of God." She asked Miranda if it was okay to use this phrase since it didn't include a verb. Miranda asked the team, and they gave their approval. When Sylvia was a child, she often heard her mother repeat this expression, and it was etched in her mind. "Did this phrase bring on a fleeting memory?" she wondered.

Simon continued to adjust the circuits and pathways. All team members were puzzled. Another four minutes elapsed.

Sylvia finally sensed something and spoke up. "Laughing or laughter is all I can come up with. And it isn't really a thought. It's more of a feeling." Miranda wrote down Sylvia's words and made note of the time.

After another five minutes elapsed, Simon threw up his hands, indicating that he was at an impasse. Sylvia still had not mentioned any other impressions.

"Let's take a break," Suzanne announced. Everyone gave a sigh of relief or exasperation as they relaxed from the mounting tension. "How long of a break?" Sharon Vogel asked.

"Let's not take the probes off of Ron and Sylvia just yet, but bring them each a cold bottle of water. Oh, and ask Nora and Miranda to come back in."

"All right." Sharon reached into the small fridge, took out two water bottles, and left the room.

The door opened to Ron and Nora's room. "We're taking a break," Sharon said as she handed Ron a water bottle. "Hang loose, Ron. So far we haven't had any success, but I think we're going to try again in a few minutes. Are you okay with that?"

"I'm here for the long haul," said Ron as he took a swig of water.

"Oh, and Nora, Dr. Myers asked you to step into the testing room for a while. I think she wants to discuss how things are going."

"Okay. Good job, Mr. Provost . . . or I mean, Ron." They both grinned as Nora and Sharon exited the room. Ron sat back in his easy chair, closed his eyes, and grinned for no apparent reason.

Nora and Miranda were briefed on what had taken place inside the testing room. Team members were asked to give their input as to what might have been the reason for the failed experiment. Everyone had an opinion, but none had any basis in fact.

When the discussion came to Nora, she shared her perspective. "You said that Sylvia mentioned a sensation of laughter. Well, I want to point out something about Ron Provost. As you all know, he was my science teacher in high school. I got to know him over two years at school. He has a certain way about him. He always brought a sense of levity and even joy to the classroom. We kids might have been having a difficult day or were dealing with issues at home, but Mr. Provost was able to give us a kind of lift. He was also very supportive and seemed to care about each one of his students. And there's something else. Suzanne, I told you that I had gone to a debate where Mr. Provost and another teacher debated the topic of evolution versus creation science." Suzanne nodded, and then added, "I know you talked about his stance on evolution, that he disagreed with it. You told me you were impressed with his presentation."

Nora continued. "Yes. He gave a very convincing argument, but that's not my point. It is quite obvious to all who know him that he takes his Christianity very seriously."

"Yeah. So?" Simon was eager for Nora to get to her point.

"Okay. So, if you consider that Mr. Provost has a kind of good-natured humor and happiness and even a peace about him and you compare that to Mrs. Ramon's more reserved manner, along with coming from a Catholic upbringing and culture, then perhaps they aren't a good match. Maybe that's why her mind wouldn't accept Ron's thoughts. But maybe Sylvia tapped into Mr. Provost's, um, temperament or something."

Suzanne interjected. "Temperament? Nora, a brain is a brain. Neuroscience does not make a distinction between cultural and differing perspectives on life, or even personality. It is simply an organ of the body. Besides, if you are suggesting that Ron's religious views aren't compatible with Sylvia's, well, they are both religious. I can't see that this has any bearing on the outcome."

Miranda spoke up. "Dr. Myers, I, too, am Catholic. I know that Sylvia was raised in a Catholic upbringing, but she wrote on her application that she had no religious affiliation. She is not a practicing Catholic and perhaps isn't even a believer. And look at the phrase she used—Mary, the mother of God. She told me she used that phrase because it was a common expression she heard from her mother growing up. No Protestant uses that expression, whether they are a believer or not. These two come from two different worldviews. Maybe Nora's onto something."

"Dr. Milton, what do you think?" Suzanne was giving consideration to Nora and Miranda's observations but wanted to get input from a close colleague.

"Like you, Dr. Myers, I have been trained to look at the brain and its connection to the body from a neurological standpoint. Humans are cognitive beings. I take the position, even in psychology, that if one can change a person's environment or experiences, and be given the right kind of medication, then the brain responds to the different stimuli. It is an organ, just like any other organ of the body."

Sharon had remained quiet but felt she needed to share her opinion. "Can I add something?" she asked.

"Certainly," Suzanne replied.

"If Nora is right, then this suggests that humans are more than just biological beings responding to certain stimuli and brain chemistry. Perhaps we are, as some would suggest, made up of body, mind, and soul, and this is . . ."

"Nonsense," interrupted Dr. Milton. "Even if this were true, how would a soul affect brain activity?"

Sharon felt shamed and hung her head, certain of her opinion and disappointed that she had not been taken seriously. Suzanne spoke up. "Whether this body and soul issue is a contributing factor or not, we might need to consider the issue of compatibility. Maybe it has something to do with the difference in composition between the male and female brains. We are pioneering an unknown frontier and need to consider untested factors. For today, let's send our volunteers home. I have some thoughts to discuss with Nora concerning bringing in another subject or two. We may also want to team Sylvia Ramon with Erin Roberts and see if that makes a difference." Everyone concurred with Suzanne's suggestion. Nora and Miranda left the room to inform Ron and Sylvia of their decision.

≈≈≈≈≈

Nora sat at a desk, combing through the many volunteer applications the study had received over the previous months. She had originally circled and made note of the various attributes each candidate brought to the table that might benefit the research study. Some candidates were more suited to being transmitters of thoughts, while others were more suitable as receivers. Nora did not want to replace Ron Provost. That may have been partially due to her bias. She knew he was an excellent choice. She was trying to find a good match for him, giving consideration to her point of observation. Dr. Myers had given Nora full rein to choose three prospects for consideration. Although Dr. Myers felt that it might be important to match same-gender brains, Nora did not believe that was a factor. She chose one male and two female applicants, purposely manipulating the chosen applicants and making sure the best compatible candidates would match Ron with a female volunteer. After all, if the study were successful, it would be important to mix and match the sexes.

One application, in particular, caught her attention. The team had interviewed this candidate but observed that she had many competing interests and felt this might cause her to be scatterbrained at the time of testing, thus being unable to focus. It also meant she might not be available at a moment's notice. Still, she seemed to be a good match for Ron Provost. They both held similar beliefs and worldviews. They were both teachers but at two separate schools. There was one distinct difference between the two. They were of different ethnicities. Ron was Caucasian. The other candidate, whose name was Natuma Nwondi, was a black woman from Uganda. Even though they came from two different cultures, both held very similar values and beliefs. Both emphasized their relationship with Jesus Christ as fundamental to how they viewed life, the values they held, and the choices they made. Nora just had a sense that this was a good match and hoped that Suzanne would agree with her assessment and choice.

CHAPTER 18

JUNE 13, 2028
3RD ATTEMPT AT THOUGHT TRANSMISSION
ROOM B11 IN THE BASEMENT OF THE NEUROSCIENCE
BUILDING OF KING'S UNIVERSITY

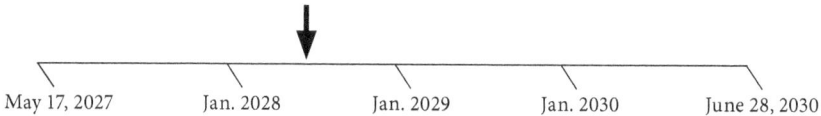

↓

| May 17, 2027 | Jan. 2028 | Jan. 2029 | Jan. 2030 | June 28, 2030 |

The first two attempts with thought transmission were met with less-than-optimal results. On their second trial run, Erin Roberts was matched up with Sylvia Ramon. It was felt that perhaps Erin might be a more suitable match with Sylvia than Ron Provost had been. Simon had corrected a few technical issues before the second attempt. The usual procedure was undertaken. On this occasion, Sylvia Ramon experienced an impression of sadness and anxiety rather than an actual thought emanating from Erin Roberts' mind. Sylvia also related a phenomenon she could not fully explain. She felt as if she had, for a brief moment, stepped out of her own consciousness. The team members questioned her in an attempt to gain some insight but were left perplexed. Sylvia said she also experienced a "change in personality," as she put it. "But only for a few seconds," she added. Dr. Myers and Dr. Milton then questioned Erin about her own sensation during the experiment. Erin admitted she was not able to fully concentrate due to the episode on the hiking trail a few days earlier, which left her feeling troubled and anxious. This was the impression Sylvia had felt coming from Erin's transmission. Dr. Myers realized there was an emotional component to their experiment, which brought valuable insight and encouragement to the team.

They decided to bring Ron Provost back for their third attempt. He was matched up with Nora's recommendation for a suitable candidate. Natuma Nwondi was brought onboard after undergoing the same scrutiny as every other volunteer on the team. During this second attempt at transmitting Ron's thoughts, he was once again not permitted to know the identity of the intended receiver. The same routine as before was taken in both rooms. Once again, Simon performed his "work of art," as he called it, on Ron's exposed scalp. Ron had become accustomed to his new look. He decided it made him appear more virile. Mona agreed that it gave him an appearance of a "tough guy," as she put it.

Ron hummed a tune as Simon worked on his scalp.

"What are you humming?" asked Simon.

"How Great Is Your Love."

"I like you, man, but can't say that I love you." Simon cracked a smile. Ron hesitated to respond. He was under strict orders from Simon not to move, so he determined not to laugh.

Simon completed attaching the last of the electrodes and then rearranged the many wires protruding from Ron's scalp that led to the testing room.

"All right, Ron, we're done." Simon once again stood back to admire his work. "Now this time we're going to change things up a bit. I'll come over the intercom and tell you if we need you to do anything different."

"Got it." Ron wasn't sure how much variation could possibly come from concentrating on a simple thought. "So Simon, I was never told what went wrong with the first attempt. What's different this time?"

"All I can tell you is that you have a different receiver than before. It's a lady again. And this time she apparently has more in common with you than the previous receiver."

Ron had no idea what Simon meant by having more in common. *"Did he mean neurologically or was it something else?"* he wondered. He didn't have a chance to ask since Simon then asked, "Do you need to go to the bathroom before we get started?" *"Simon, the incessant jokester,"* thought Ron. Simon immediately snickered, amused with his own comedic ways. "Adios," proclaimed Simon as he turned and exited the room.

Nora walked into the room toting her usual tablet. She asked for Ron's chosen thought and then laughed as she wrote down what he said.

"Here we go, Ron," she commented as she situated herself in her straight-back chair. "How come you get the comfy one?" she asked Ron.

"Hey, I earned this seat, my dear."

"Yea, I guess you did." Nora was receiving instructions in her earbud as well as on her tablet. "All right, here we go."

In another room, Natuma, the receiver, had already been prepped for the experiment. Although she had been briefed about what was expected of her and the purpose of today's event, this was her first experience with the study. She was fully accepting of all that was required of her, preferring a fully shaved head over the option of selected shaved areas only. African head wraps were a popular style in her home country of Uganda. She had been living in Ontario for the past two years, having come over when the conditions of her beloved home country had forced her family to flee. She loved Canada and was looking forward to gaining citizenship. She was offered and accepted a teaching position at a local elementary school. She felt blessed.

Miranda Gomez was her room supervisor for the day. "All right, before we get started, Ms. Nwondi, I'll remind you to focus on a short common phrase you regularly use or have heard. It doesn't even have to be an English phrase if you prefer."

"Oh, I did not know that," replied Natuma. "Good. Yes, I know the words I will focus on."

"Great. That's great. May I ask what is the phrase you have chosen?"

"Mungu ni mwema."

"Could you spell that please?" Natuma gave her the spelling and then repeated the phrase.

"Oh, I love the way you say that," replied Miranda. "What does it mean?"

"God is good." Natuma broadened her smile as she saw Miranda's look of approval.

"Very good, Ms. Nwondi. Now what will happen is . . ." Miranda was cut short by Natuma.

"I am sorry to interrupt, Ms. Gomez. Please just call me Natuma. And may I call you Miranda?"

"Oh, of course. I see no harm." Miranda nodded as Natuma once more gave her a broad smile. "So anyway, what will happen is that after you begin repeating your phrase over and over to yourself in your mind, every so many seconds, Simon will open up a line connecting your brain with that of our transmitter. If we are successful, you will receive the sensation of another thought entering your mind. We found from our previous attempt at doing this that you might also receive an emotional response. In other words, the transmitter's emotional state may come across your own mind. Do you understand?"

"Do you mean that I might actually experience the essence of this person's very being on the other end? Is this true?"

Miranda leaned into Natuma and whispered, "Well, between you and me, I suppose that's another way of putting it." Miranda was hoping this admission did not cause anxious thoughts or anxiety for Natuma. Instead, Natuma remarked, "That is truly remarkable! I am very much looking forward to this experiment."

Miranda was relieved. The previous attempt between Erin and Sylvia had provided insight into implementing necessary changes, but the team was hoping to transmit a thought, even if an emotional response accompanied the thought. Miranda did not tell Natuma that she had been chosen due to similarities between her and Ron's spiritual beliefs or worldviews. The cultural differences concerned everyone on the team, but they realized these were issues that would eventually have to be overcome as they went forward in the study.

Simon came over the intercom. "We're ready on our end."

The procedure from the previous attempt was kept in place—15 seconds off and five seconds on.

"We are starting . . . now." Both rooms heard Simon's words.

Suzanne had been excited at the commencement of their previous two attempts. This time, the excitement was replaced by anxiety. She hoped that this compatibility modification would bring the success they needed. She glanced over at Randall Milton who was staring at the screen watching the sine waves on the EEG monitor and the neurotransmission pathways on the other. "They seem consistent on both ends," he uttered to Simon. "Let's give it the five seconds."

Ron had been slowly and succinctly repeating the phrase over and over again in his mind. He tried not to think of anything other than those words.

Simon opened the transmission line.

"Oh!" Natuma was startled by what suddenly took place in her mind. Miranda did not want to break her concentration, so she said nothing.

Simon closed the transmission gate and waited 15 seconds. He glanced up at Dr. Milton and then Suzanne. "Again," Randall Milton said. Simon once more opened the transmission line.

"Oh my! I'm getting something."

Everyone in the test room waited with anxious anticipation at what Natuma would say next. Simon once more closed the gateway for 15 seconds.

"What? What?" Suzanne made a gesturing motion with her arms as she listened.

"Thirteen, 14, 15 . . ." Simon opened the transmission line.

Natuma once again gave a startled response. She broke protocol and asked, "Could you transmit it once more for a bit longer this time?" She then tried to concentrate once more on her own chosen thought. Simon looked at Dr. Milton and Dr. Myers for approval to do as she asked.

"Yes, yes, that's fine," said Suzanne. The next 15 seconds crept by for what seemed an eternity to those in the room. Simon flipped the switch. He allowed it to remain open this time for two additional seconds.

Natuma began to laugh. "I think I know. This is remarkable!" she exclaimed. Miranda spoke up this time. "What is it, Natuma? What is your impression?"

"I do not know what it means. An open box?"

Miranda asked the testing room. "Was that it?" The outpouring of excitement and cheers overpowered her request. They were leaping with joy. Suzanne realized she needed to open her communication line and speak to Miranda. "Ask her what kind of box."

Miranda gently asked, "What kind of box is it, Natuma?"

"I do not know the word. A panning door . . . an open box?"

Suzanne clasped her fists in front of her mouth and then opened the intercom to Miranda and Natuma's room. "Natuma, tell us exactly . . . I mean precisely the thought that came to your mind."

Natuma turned to face Miranda. "Pan door box? Pan door box open? Is that right?" Miranda looked intently at Natuma and asked, "Do you mean Pandora's box opened?"

"Yes. Yes. That is it!" Miranda, Natuma, Ron, and Nora heard hoopla coming from down the hallway. Simon opened the intercom to Ron and Nora's room and excitedly declared, "It worked. Hey, buddy, it actually worked!"

CHAPTER 19

JUNE 11, 2030
GENEVA CONFERENCE AUDITORIUM AS RON PROVOST CONCLUDES HIS PRESENTATION

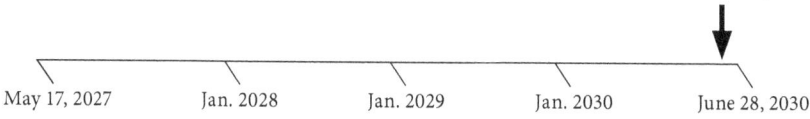

| May 17, 2027 | Jan. 2028 | Jan. 2029 | Jan. 2030 | June 28, 2030 |

Upon hearing this portion of Ron's story, the conference room crowd erupted in cheers and applause. Ron, too, began to laugh uncontrollably as he looked over at the rest of the team who were joining in the ovation. He turned once more to face the audience. "But folks, as my cousin from Texas used to say, 'You ain't heard nothin' yet!' I think I had better turn it back over to Dr. Myers at this time." He walked over to the team and sat down as they slapped him on the back and congratulated him on his experience on that commemorative day.

Suzanne walked to the podium. "What a story, huh?" The audience once again gave an approving response. I am sorry that Natuma Nwondi was not able to join us today. She is such a delightful person. She played a major role in our success." And we must also recognize Erin Roberts and Sylvia Ramon who presented to us an unexpected dimension to thought transmission. It seems we tapped into not only the thoughts of a person but perhaps their very soul, if I can be so bold." Members of the Thought

Transmission team were surprised by this unexpected declaration by Dr. Myers. The soul? They glanced around at one another. Each shrugged. Suzanne hesitated for a moment. "Well . . . so . . . we accomplished what we set out to do. But this was only the beginning. Our journey had only just begun." She added mockingly, "You ain't seen nothin' yet."

She looked at Ron who was pointing his finger at her. "Our initial success might be compared to the discovery of the wheel. What use is a wheel if it is not developed into a useful mode of transportation? In the same way, simple thoughts consisting of a short phrase would never grant our intended benefit to medical, psychological, and neurological science. We knew we had a long way to go. Let me recount for you further developments along our road of discovery. Over the ensuing months, we encountered even more anomalies through the transmission of thoughts. The receivers continued to speak of a sensation of departure from their own consciousness as well as taking on an entirely different personality for only brief moments in time. We knew we needed to nail down the cause of these sensations, but we also encountered a roadblock. We were never able to transmit more than a basic two- or three-word thought. We had reached a standstill.

CHAPTER 20

SEPTEMBER 8, 2028
ROOM B11 OF THE NEUROSCIENCE BUILDING AT KING'S UNIVERSITY / THE THOUGHT TRANSMISSION TEAM REACHES AN IMPASSE AND DISCUSSES WAYS TO MOVE FORWARD WITH THE STUDY

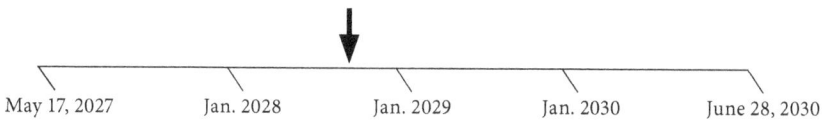

↓

| May 17, 2027 | Jan. 2028 | Jan. 2029 | Jan. 2030 | June 28, 2030 |

A pot of coffee in the corner of the conference room had grown cold. The Thought Transmission team sat around the table with an assortment of tablets, laptops, and empty coffee cups. The team's progress had come to an impasse. In addition to their initial success with Ron and Natuma, they continued to make improvements and refine the procedure. Other volunteers were also able to consistently transmit and receive thoughts, but the results were still rudimentary. Transmitting purely austere thoughts would never give them the results they needed to produce a procedure neurologically useful to medical science. Several attempts had been made to transmit more complex thoughts but were always met with failure. The consensus was that it would be necessary to slow down the transmitter's neurotransmission of thoughts to successfully map them before sending them on to the receiver. Every suggestion was met with skepticism by others on the team. Simon had remained mostly silent throughout the meeting. He was listening intently to everyone's comments and finally spoke up.

"I'm not so sure that slowing down neurotransmission activity is the answer. We need to face the fact that there is an enormous amount of activity going on in the brain. The data we are able to collect from a few dozen electrodes just isn't going to cut it. And even the most sophisticated computer cannot compete with the marvels of this four-pound mass of tissue we all have between our ears."

Dr. Randall Milton interrupted. "You're not helping the situation, Simon. You're only compounding the problem." Dr. Milton's manner was often abrupt and intimidating, which Simon found difficult to overcome.

"Yea, I know. But let me throw this out there. The electrodes we use have come a long way since even a few years ago. They're less than a millimeter in diameter. I believe I can design and build a skull cap made from translucent rubber and then plant literally hundreds of these electrodes into it. We've only been using, like I said, a couple dozen electrodes up to this point. The computer program I'm using isn't designed to handle more than that."

"So now we're limited by the computer software?" asked Dr. Myers.

"Not necessarily." Simon's thoughts were racing as he spoke. "Here's another thought. We're dealing with 3-D material, the human brain. We are limited by what we see on our computer monitors. Even though we can manipulate the image to see all sides, I think it would help us enormously if we had an actual 3-D model of what's taking place in our subject's brain. We could then get a better grasp on the neurological pathways."

Dr. Milton interjected. "Are you suggesting a neuromorphic engineered model? What kind of material would be used?"

Simon nodded his head as he was contemplating his answer. "Here's where I think we need to bring onboard the physics department. This is out of my area of expertise. But I'm thinking, with their help, we could build a sizable model of the human brain that would actually mimic brain activity. Are you guys following me?"

"What would this model consist of?" Dr. Milton was insistent on getting an answer.

Dr. Suzanne Myers jumped in. "And that still doesn't answer the software problem."

"I'm coming to that." Simon paused long enough to gather his thoughts.

"To answer your question first, Dr. Milton, I'm thinking that our friends over in the physics department can tell us what kind of substance this would take. The exterior would be transparent, of course, but I'm thinking it might be filled with the same material used in plasma TVs. Do you remember those first-generation flat screens from about 40 years ago?"

"A what TV?" Nora asked.

"Before your time. Mine, too, for that matter. So anyway, picture this. We've got the brain electrodes, hundreds of them, hooked into this model of the brain that is lighting up wherever we see a neurotransmission pathway, just like what is going on inside our subject transmitter's brain. That would give us an enormous advantage over simply viewing the activity on a two-dimensional computer monitor." Simon could see the disgruntled look on Randall Milton's face, but he also detected optimism coming from Suzanne Myers. "It can be done. Trust me. But again, we need to get at least one expert from physics to jump in."

"And I have to ask again. What about the data download?" Suzanne was becoming optimistic but was trying to consider any factors that might pose a problem somewhere down the road.

"Dr. Myers, think of it like this. Imagine a 100-lane highway containing lots of cars. That's like our brain activity, okay?" He observed a look of comprehension on each face. "Now what we have been trying to do is narrow those 100 lanes of traffic down to only two lanes and send the two lanes down the road, expecting them to turn back into a 100-lane highway. So, what I am proposing is that we keep the 100-lane highway intact but make them, along with the cars on it, smaller."

"You're losing us, Simon," said Dr. Myers.

"All right, it's like this. Satellites pick up images of all this traffic on Earth and then beam it down to us in a form we can comprehend. That's part of what GPS does on our phones. Right? So this model I'm proposing would be like a satellite. It receives the input from the transmitter's brain and then changes it to another format before sending it on to our computer. Meanwhile, we would be able to view and even record the brain activity inside the model. From the model, the signal is passed on to the computer where it can be recorded and played back. We can also pause the image on the computer, if necessary, and then send it to the receiver."

There was a momentary silence in the room as everyone looked around the table to see who was going to speak next. Finally, Dr. Myers spoke up. "So, I think Simon might be onto something. How about you, Randall?"

"I'm thinking this sounds way outside of our purview." He then added, "and expensive."

"All right, what about bringing someone from the physics department onboard?" Suzanne felt this would have to be the first line of consideration. "Is everyone in favor of doing that?"

Everyone nodded in agreement, mostly due to the hope that this would move things along and end this endlessly long day.

"Then it's settled," Suzanne turned to Simon. "Simon, do you know anyone over in that department who can help us?"

"I know just the guy. His name is Andreas Grisham. He's a good friend of mine. He has done studies with biomorphic and neuromorphic engineering. His emphasis is on both chemical and physical science. Andreas is a typical science nerd. He's super smart and gets things done. And he can catch things the rest of us just don't see. He's our man." Simon rose from his seat, confident that his suggestion would be enthusiastically received. He refilled his cup and grimaced as he took a swig. "Oh man, this stuff's nasty."

Suzanne also stood. "So once more, we're all in agreement that we need to take this course of action?" Everyone nodded in agreement. "Now we need to discuss cost." A collective groan came from everyone in the room. "All right, I can see we're all ready to call it a day. We'll deal with that later. Let's reconvene this time next week. That should give Simon enough time to speak with Andreas. Simon, I'm curious. Does he have his Ph.D.?"

"Nah, I don't think so. He's just a really smart nerd who knows his stuff."

"Well, I'm sure that's fine if you think he's our go-to man."

Simon threw his foam coffee cup in the trash as he turned to face Suzanne. "He is." Simon was becoming impatient. "Hey, my wife needs me to pick up some stuff from the store. Are we finished?"

"Yes, Simon. You can go on home." Suzanne gave him and the rest of the team a nod, a smile, and a wave of her hand as Simon rushed through the door. One by one the others filed through the door, leaving Suzanne alone with her thoughts. As in earlier days, the what-ifs continued to haunt her. They might move forward with Simon's vision, but at what cost? *"What if we fail?"* she thought. *"We cannot merely skim the surface of this newfound discovery. Otherwise,* we will find ourselves back to a dog-and-pony show." She would have to ask for more funding. And then what if they failed to advance their study to an appropriate level of functionality? She would have to answer not only to the Weinberg Institute but to the entire institution of science. The year would soon be coming to a close. She already had her eye on the Science Conference in Geneva that was less than two years away. They had a lot of work to do between now and then. She decided to remain positive in her outlook. *"We will succeed,"* she confidently told herself. "We must succeed," she said aloud.

CHAPTER 21

SATURDAY, SEPTEMBER 30, 2028
HOME OF RON AND MONA PROVOST

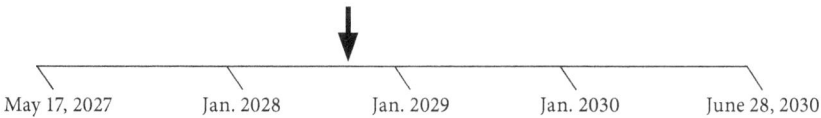

May 17, 2027   Jan. 2028   Jan. 2029   Jan. 2030   June 28, 2030

"Why don't we invite Dr. Myers to our home for Thanksgiving?" Mona suggested, agreeing with Ron that they should form a relationship with Dr. Myers. Ron was aware that the Thought Transmission study had detected new insight into the nature of humankind. He also knew that Dr. Myers was struggling with this discovery that challenged her own naturalistic views. It was becoming more and more apparent that the human condition encompassed much more than mere biological and neurological beings. Ron felt these recent developments might cause Suzanne to consider a biblical worldview. But Ron's motivation was not just that Suzanne would consider changing her worldview. He wanted to share the gospel with this new colleague he had grown to love and appreciate. He had long ago memorized Romans 1:16: "For I am not ashamed of the gospel, for it is the power of God for salvation to everyone who believes." Ron wanted Suzanne to realize that it was Jesus, the Son of God, who paid the penalty for our sin and rebellion against our holy God. He wanted her to receive a restored relationship and peace with her heavenly Father. How could he ignore the obvious leading and preparation by the Holy Spirit to bring him into this Thought Transmission study for the very purpose of sharing God's love? He could not continue to set aside this charge to share the good news and bring glory to his heavenly Father. Ron simply needed to be God's mouthpiece. The Lord Himself was preparing Suzanne's heart and mind to trust Him. Ron began looking for an opportunity to build a loving and respectful relationship with Suzanne and to then be obedient to share this good news. His desire was that all the Thought Transmission team would recognize this new life offered by their Creator. Ron saw the big picture unfolding before him.

"That's a great idea, Hon." Ron was thrilled with Mona's suggestion to invite Suzanne to their home for Thanksgiving. "I know she is single, but she may have family in the area. She might just accept the invite. Besides, we don't necessarily have to invite her on Thanksgiving Day. It's on the 9th this year, correct?"

Mona checked the calendar. "Yes, Monday the 9th.."

"And this just occurred to me. I know she has relatives in America, so she may be planning to celebrate there in November."

"We won't know unless we invite her," Mona replied. "How about you give her a call? Or better yet, how about we both call her on speaker phone?"

"Let's call her this evening, maybe around 7:30 p.m." Ron knew that Suzanne often put in late hours at the university, even on a Saturday. The Canadian Thanksgiving celebration was a little over a week away.

"All right," Mona agreed. "Meanwhile I'll pick up Brenda from my folks' house. Jeremy and Trevor are at hockey practice. They finish up around 5:00 p.m. Do you mind?"

"I'll pick them up and pizza, too, while I'm out." Saturday was typically pizza night at the Provost home.

Sheldon heard "pizza" and gave a bark of approval.

≈≈≈≈≈

130

Suzanne Myers was completing a report on the progress of the Thought Transmission project. By now the team could no longer deny the fact that there were other factors beyond the transference of rudimentary thoughts. The receivers experienced not just a neurological and emotional component coming from the transmission but something they could not fully explain. They spoke of "losing themselves" and "taking on another persona." If it were true that other attributes of the transmitter were being conveyed to the receiver, then how was she to interpret these experiences and explain them in terms of neurological processes? Suzanne was certainly aware of the billions of characteristics that come into play in forming the unique personality of an individual. Some of these differences could be explained by DNA, heredity, environmental factors, social interaction, relationships, or even differences in the structure of the brain. Other factors such as biological and electrochemical components influence our unique persona. "*So how is it that these factors are being transferred from one individual to another simply by transmitting neurotransmission pathways?*" she thought. Suzanne did not mind utilizing the term *soul* in reference to each individual's unique personality and temperament. But she did not view the soul of an individual in the stereotypical religious context.

Suzanne's phone rang. She saw that it was Ron Provost calling. "Hello, Mr. Provost. To what do I owe the pleasure?"

"Hi, Dr. Myers. My wife, Mona, and I were just talking about you, and . . ."

"Oh?" Ron's statement caught Suzanne by surprise. "And were they good thoughts or . . ."

"Absolutely. We want to invite you over to our house for Thanksgiving. We didn't know if you had any other plans, but we wanted to check."

Mona's voice suddenly came over the line. "Mona here, Dr. Myers. Yes, we would love to have you join our family on the 9th."

Suzanne could find no reason to deny the offer and welcomed the invitation. "I can see no reason why I can't make it to your house on the 9th. So yes, I would be delighted."

Ron and Mona both chimed in. "Great!" Mona then added, "Are there any dietary restrictions?"

"No, not at all. After all, it's a Thanksgiving meal. We get to make exceptions on that day, right?" They all laughed.

Mona, Ron, and Suzanne discussed some of the team's progress and unexpected findings. Upon ending the call, Suzanne thought to herself that perhaps Ron and Mona might add some insight into these recent anomalies. She welcomed the chance to interact. The early stages of a bond of lasting friendship were in the making.

OCTOBER 9, 2028
CANADIAN THANKSGIVING DAY HOME OF RON AND MONA PROVOST

↓

May 17, 2027   Jan. 2028   Jan. 2029   Jan. 2030   June 28, 2030

Sheldon, the four-legged, floppy-eared door barker alerted the Provost family of the visitor at their door.

Mona was in the kitchen. "Ron, would you get . . ."

"On it," came the reply. Ron opened the front door. "Dr. Myers. You're right on time. Come in." Ron motioned their guest into the foyer.

Mona unfurled her apron and set it on the kitchen counter as she hurried to the foyer. "Dr. Myers, it's a pleasure to finally meet you."

"And you. Oh, and please call me Suzanne." She then turned to Ron. "And you. too, Ron."

Ron escorted Suzanne past Sheldon who eagerly greeted his newfound friend. "And who is this?" Suzanne asked as Sheldon circled in excitement.

"Suzanne, meet Sheldon." Ron knew he could always count on Sheldon to greet their visitors with enthusiasm. Suzanne did not have a pet of her own due to her busy schedule, but she loved dogs nevertheless. Jeremy, Brenda, and Trevor filed into the room and were promptly introduced.

"Dinner is almost ready. If you need to freshen up, Suzanne, the restroom is down the hall." Mona turned her attention to the kids. "Trevor, you and Brenda please set out the silver. And be sure to wash your hands first. Jeremy, you take Sheldon to the backyard, please."

"Have a seat, Suzanne." Ron motioned her to the sofa.

A ding was heard coming from the kitchen. "If you'll excuse me, I've got rolls to take out of the oven, and then we can move on into the dining room." Mona left the duo as she hurried away.

"Do you need any help, Hon?" Ron called out as she left the room. Suzanne, too, spoke up. "Yes, are you sure you don't need my help, Mona?" Suzanne stood as she made the offer.

"No, thanks. I just need to get the rolls out and set dinner on the table. Please, just make yourself comfortable."

Suzanne sat back down and faced Ron. "I'm so glad to get to meet Mona and the children. Thank you for inviting me."

Ron sat across from Suzanne. This relaxed atmosphere was actually causing him a bit of tension. He was more at ease teaching students the marvels of science, coaching soccer, or performing prescribed duties. Regardless, he found that as long as he focused on another person's needs rather than his own, he was able to interact and help others feel at ease. Doing so helped relieve his own tension.

"Mona and I have wanted to get together with you for some time. Me especially. I want to find out more about Suzanne beyond the Doctor of Neuroscience."

"Not much to tell, really."

"I'm sure there's more to you than your vocational pursuits."

Suzanne did not have a chance to respond as Mona walked back into the den and announced, "Everyone come to the table."

The children sat down at their previously prescribed spots. Ron sat at the head with Mona to his right and Jeremy to his left. Suzanne was offered a chair next to Mona. Trevor and Brenda rounded out the other end of the table. Normally the family held hands as Ron gave thanks. Not wanting Suzanne to feel uncomfortable, he gave a slight shake of his head toward the children, indicating they would forego this hand-holding ritual.

"I'll say grace," Ron announced. He bowed his head and offered a typical invocation of thanksgiving. He then added a special thanks to God for allowing Suzanne to join them on this special feast day. Suzanne had not grown up with this custom but was always respectful whenever prayers were voiced before meals. Trevor rounded out the prayer by saying, "Good food, good meat, good God, let's eat!"

Ron calmly gave a reprimand. "Trevor, that's enough. We show our Maker and Provider honor and respect at this house. You know better than that."

"Sorry, Dad," Trevor replied as he filled his mouth with dressing.

Suzanne smiled at Trevor. She was enjoying watching the family interaction. She had no children of her own. Although she had dated several men over the years, she never married. She had grown accustomed to the single life. She felt a twinge of regret from time to time, but the feeling soon passed. She was comfortable with her status in life.

During the meal, Mona asked Suzanne where she had grown up.

"I'm originally from San Francisco," she responded.

"Where is that?" asked Brenda.

Jeremy interjected, "California, of course." Mona gave him a stern look.

Suzanne replied to Brenda's question. "Yes, it's in the state of California. Do you know where California is, Brenda?"

"Sure do. Lots of movies are made there."

"That's right. San Francisco overlooks the Pacific Ocean. It is a very beautiful city."

"It has lots of earthquakes from what I hear," Trevor noted.

"Well, yes. Some are not very big. Most people don't even feel them. But they have had several large ones too. I don't remember too much about San Francisco because my father moved us to Dallas, Texas, when I was about your age, Brenda. I lived there until I went to college. I ended up at King's University in Toronto for my graduate studies. I've been here in Toronto ever since."

Jeremy sat across from Suzanne. "Dr. Myers, how do you say p-e-c-a-n?" he asked.

"Pecan, with the emphasis on the 'con.' How do you say it, Jeremy?"

Trevor spoke before Jeremy had a chance to respond. "He says pee-can."

"I can speak for myself, Trevor. But yeah, that's the way we all say it in this family."

"I now live in Toronto, so yes, I've noticed that's the way it's pronounced here. I see the pee-can pie at your end of the table, Trevor." Suzanne mimicked the Toronto accent as she asked for a slice of pee-can pie. "Are you going to share it?"

"Not before I get a piece," interrupted Ron as he reached for the pie plate.

He was too late as Brenda intercepted his reach. "Dad, that's sooo rude," said Brenda as she swiped a piece for herself before passing it on to Suzanne who took a slice and then passed it over to Mona.

"Hey!" exclaimed Ron.

Mona spoke up. "Suzanne, if you want a piece of pecan pie, you've got to grab it quickly in this family." Everyone laughed.

Suzanne enjoyed interacting with the Provost children. She noticed how everyone in the family seemed to show mutual respect for one another. She recognized that this was an attribute missing in many of today's families. She often wondered what kind of cultural, environmental, familial, and even hereditary factors came into play to form family dynamics.

After dinner, everyone convened in the den. As they sat down, Mona remarked, "Excuse me just a moment while I say a brief hello to my parents. She made the call to her folks who lived in Ottawa. After a brief greeting, she handed the phone to Jeremy. "Here, kids, say hello to Gramma and Granddad." She handed them the phone and ushered them into the study.

"I apologize," said Mona. "I just wanted to occupy the kids while we visit a bit longer."

Ron had prepared coffee during the meal and brought the pot and cups into the den. "Who wants coffee?" Both ladies accepted the invitation. "I like mine straight," added Ron. Mona and Suzanne helped themselves to the creamer and sweeteners.

Suzanne settled into her place on the sofa. "Your children are sweet. I have to congratulate you on bringing them up so well."

Mona took a sip of coffee and then responded, "Thank you. We've certainly been blessed, and we try to instruct them and model for them the right way to treat others. But I have to tell you that . . ."

"God's grace." Ron immediately recognized his overt interception. "Oh, I'm sorry, Hon. I shouldn't have interrupted."

Suzanne was listening to Mona but was a bit startled by Ron's outburst.

"Yes, that's what I was going to point out," added Mona. "It's mostly the grace of God that's at play here."

"What do you mean?" Suzanne asked.

Ron looked toward Mona, expecting an answer, and remained silent. Mona took another sip of coffee and then set it down on the side table. "As you've probably picked up, Ron and I are followers of Christ. That means we recognize that we do not have all the right answers. We need God's grace to lead us and guard against all the harmful influences coming against our family. We trust Him, even if things do not always turn out as we hoped."

"Oh, I'm sure if you provide them the right environment and education, they will turn out just fine. I commend you both on the good example you are setting." Suzanne did not concur with the God factor.

Ron prayed silently to himself, *"Give me gracious words and a heart of compassion."* He added, "Like Mona said, we try to do our best to raise them right, but even then, we have no guarantee of what the future holds. And I'm not talking necessarily about their behavior but what will take place in their heart. Will they have a heart of kindness and consideration toward others or live solely for their own self-interests?"

Suzanne nodded as she took another sip of coffee. She did not want to disagree with Ron but knew from experience that cognitive behavioral therapy was a sure way to correct wrong thinking.

Mona, not wanting the conversation to become too philosophical, asked Suzanne, "You mentioned living in San Francisco and then moving to Dallas. What did your father do for a living?"

"He worked in the biotech industry in the late 1970s, right when biotechnology was first getting started. His company moved us to Dallas as the industry grew."

Ron was curious. "From San Francisco to Dallas and then to Ontario. That's a lot of culture change, wouldn't you say?"

"Oh yes. And climate too."

Mona stepped into the conversation. "Were your parents more comfortable living in San Francisco or Dallas?"

"They both grew up in California and much preferred the climate there. Dallas is unbearable in the summer months. Actually, my parents moved to St. Louis about the same time I started attending school in Toronto. My father took a job there. That's where I usually go for Thanksgiving in November. Now it's my turn," announced Suzanne. "Tell me how you two met."

Ron and Mona looked at one another and laughed. Mona spoke first. "Our story probably isn't that much different than most. We both attended college at Ontario Tech University in Oshawa, Ontario."

Ron continued. "She was in social sciences and humanities, and I was in the science department."

"How did you two meet?" Suzanne asked.

Ron gave Mona the floor for this one. "Interestingly enough, we met at a church we both attended while in school."

"King Street Community Church," Ron pointed out. "We found we both had a desire to walk with the Lord. I wasn't there looking for a wife but found that Mona and I seemed to be headed in the same direction."

"Oh, that's nice."

Ron wanted to steer the conversation back to matters pertaining to the Christian worldview. "Suzanne, I know you take a naturalistic view of the world. Correct?"

"Pretty much, yes."

"Can I ask you a question?"

"Of course."

"What is the source of evil in your opinion? And how would you define it?"

"From a naturalistic standpoint, I would agree with others who say that evil is a byproduct of our evolutionary past. In the pursuit of survival, we have had to fight just to exist. I believe that one day we can all overcome these evil tendencies." Suzanne was comfortable stating this explanation, but Ron could sense she was not coming from her heart but just relating the tenets of a naturalistic worldview.

Before Ron could respond, Mona asked, "Suzanne, is that truly what you believe?"

Suzanne was caught off guard by this honest question. "Well, to be quite honest, I really haven't dwelled much on the issue." Suzanne had the utmost respect for these two new friends. But she was not so naive that she didn't pick up on the obvious attempt by Ron and Mona to steer the conversation in a religious direction. She would turn the question back to them. "So where would you say evil comes from?"

Ron looked at Mona who just mouthed, "Go ahead."

"Actually, I think we can both agree that evil is very much apparent in our world. We see it everywhere. And as far back as history shows, it's always been with us. Right?"

"Yes. I agree."

"Where we might differ is on its source. As you know, Mona and I hold to a Christian worldview. So if you would allow me, I'll explain it from a biblical viewpoint."

"That's fine. That's one perspective among many."

"All right. Evil, from a biblical standpoint, is simply referred to as sin. And sin is something that everyone who has ever been born, except for one person, has deep within themselves. Because of our sin, we face

God's wrath and His judgment against our sin. We are all guilty before this perfect and holy God. If we do not use the biblical definition of sin and judgment, then humanity can define it in any way it wants. It ends up being determined by society's definition of right and wrong. And so, for instance, from the perspective of Nazi Germany, their right was to exterminate the Jewish people. Or think about the issue of slavery. Over 600,000 Americans lost their lives as a nation tried to determine what was right and wrong."

Suzanne interjected. "What about Christianity itself? The church murdered hundreds in the name of God. And even in the Bible, God told people to kill others while at the same time saying it was wrong to kill."

Mona looked at Ron, knowing this is one of the biggest objections to Christianity. He continued. "I won't defend or try to explain such things. Awful things have certainly been committed in the name of God. But what I will point out is that we humans are sinners by nature and have done many atrocious acts that always come from a heart of sin. In other words, it is our nature to sin and rebel against our holy God. Not only that, but all of us are, as you said, trying to survive in a world that has been tainted by this malady of sin. We are often controlled by our lust for selfish desires and ambition. We hurt others in an attempt to get our own way. None of us, Christian or not, can say we are without sin. It is glaringly obvious, and it is tragic."

"But," Mona interjected, "there is hope. Suzanne, God knows we are messed up sinners. I won't go into how this all came about. That could be another topic for another day. But because He is perfect and holy, He cannot tolerate sin. It goes against God's very nature. And God made it clear in the Bible that we are guilty and separated from Him because of this inward sin."

"I admit I've made mistakes, but I won't admit that I am a terrible, evil person." Suzanne felt she needed to justify herself. "You seem to have a bleak view of people in general. I believe people are generally good by nature. If there is a God, then I can see why He would send an evil person to hell, I suppose. But I don't understand why He even allows evil to begin with."

Brenda ran into the room. "Dad, Trevor won't give me the remote. I had it first, and he took it. Tell him to give it back." Ron stood to address the sudden ordeal. Instead, Mona motioned him to sit back down. "I'll take care of this," she offered as she ushered Brenda back into the study.

Ron started to mention the evidence for the self-centeredness of humanity that had just been on display but decided against it. Instead, he directed his attention back to Suzanne. "I'll address that in a minute." He picked up the pot of coffee. "First, can I fill your cup?" Suzanne nodded. "Sure, I'll have some more." Mona walked back in as Ron then pointed the pot toward her. She shook her head.

Ron continued to speak as he poured more coffee into Suzanne's cup. "The Bible doesn't distinguish between degrees of sin so much as it states that we are all guilty of rebelling against God's righteous ways. It says that even one sin is enough to make us guilty and face God's judgment. As to why God allows evil, well, since evil is obvious in the world, then how should God respond? Since we are all guilty, then He could just wipe us all out, I suppose. In fact, just as you pointed out, God intervened in the affairs of mankind, as we read in Scripture. Sometimes He did so in what appears to be harsh ways, at least from a human perspective. Even though we may interpret God as unjust, everything He does comes from love. God is defined by love. So what's the solution? Here's the catch. God didn't create us to be like robots who obey Him from obligation. No. He provided us the opportunity to love and honor Him from a heart of gratitude and trust. But again, we are all born with a nature that does not willingly love and obey. So that brings us right back to the hopeless state we find ourselves in."

"But Mona, you said there is hope. Where's the hope?"

Mona had waited for the opportunity to speak of God's hope. "I'm glad you asked. Hope comes through God's good plan to restore us back to Him. God is eager to forgive, but His justice cannot overlook our sin. He didn't just leave us in this hopeless state. God had a rescue plan to free us from sin's control. In the Old Testament of the Bible, many prophecies portray a coming Messiah. Even the prophets themselves did not have a full picture or understand the mission of this Messiah.

They knew that this Messiah was supposed to restore Israel and save them from their enemies, but they really didn't fully grasp the bigger implications of the hope this Messiah would bring."

"You're talking about Jesus, aren't you?" Suzanne was wondering when Jesus would be brought up in the conversation.

Both Ron and Mona replied, "That's right." Mona then continued. "Jesus fulfilled all these prophecies. When He came into the world, He began to preach a message about the kingdom of God. He wasn't just some traveling rabbi teaching about God. He performed miracles. He even showed power over nature and the elements."

"I find it hard to buy into all that."

Ron interjected. "I understand your hesitancy, Suzanne. But I also want to ask you to hear the rest of the story. The miracles had a purpose. They showed that Jesus was actually divine. He even said that He and the Father were one. He admitted that the purpose of the miracles was to bring validity to that fact."

"Now you're expecting me to just accept those stories in the Bible as fact. Not only do I have trouble believing in a God who reigns over everything and became a man ages ago, I really can't see the relevance of the Bible. Most of those stories sound more like fairy tales to me. I can't just accept the Bible as coming from God. After all, men wrote it. And I'm sure it must have changed over the centuries."

Ron looked at Mona, who urged him to continue. "There are answers to your concerns. But first, let me tell you about the biggest miracle of all."

"What was that?"

"As you know, Jesus was crucified. There is plenty of testimony to that fact. The main reason He was crucified, from a human standpoint, was that He claimed equality with God. Despite all the evidence, fulfilled prophecy, miracles, and His message, the religious elite saw Him as a threat to Jewish tradition. They saw Him as a heretic. After all, He claimed equality with God. I, too, might have agreed with them at the time. That's an outlandish claim." Ron saw Suzanne nod in agreement. Ron continued. "So they had Him crucified. But from God's standpoint, something else was behind the crucifixion. It, too, was prophesied. The prophet Isaiah wrote a message from God 700 years or so before the birth of Jesus. The 53rd chapter of the book of Isaiah contains a powerful prophecy that Jesus fulfilled right before the eyes of those who witnessed His crucifixion. They were blind to that message. I'm going to challenge you, Suzanne, to read it for yourself. That prophecy in Isaiah and other prophetic words found elsewhere in the Old Testament contains the greatest message and miracle of all."

Suzanne knew where Ron was leading. "I know what you are going to say. You are going to tell me He came back to life. Right?"

Mona had been sitting back listening to Ron relate the gospel message. She decided to step in. "Right! Now here's the real reason Jesus was crucified. He gave His life. It wasn't taken from Him. He willingly went to the cross. He did that to buy us back from sin's hold on our hearts and lives. A price had to be paid. The verdict is in. All of humanity is guilty. We all deserve God's punishment. But Jesus, as God, could pay that price. He never sinned. He perfectly obeyed God the Father. He was the only person who ever did so. But as God's Son, having been born from the Spirit of God but fully human as well, He represents all of humanity before the Father. That meant God's justice was met. It also means that God's mercy could now be given to all who would place their trust in that price Jesus made on our behalf. This is the hope I mentioned earlier. God offers forgiveness, but it has to come through Jesus who became our mediator before the Father. All other religions state that forgiveness can only come through earning God's favor. Not Christianity. We must trust in the work of Christ alone for salvation."

Suzanne was listening to Ron and Mona intently but was still unsure of their message. She felt a bit uncomfortable at this point. She knew if she voiced another objection that these two would probably have an answer for her. Ron and Mona both could sense Suzanne's discomfort.

Ron knew this good news message would penetrate a person's heart in one of two ways. Either someone would be convicted of their own rebellion against God or they might continue to reject God's plan of salvation. Ron was about to speak when Mona intervened.

"Suzanne, I know we've laid some heavy stuff on you tonight. Please know that Ron and I love you. We have come to appreciate you for who you are. Ron has spoken often of his respect and admiration of you. He believes this study you and the team members are involved in is opening doors to huge opportunities. Ron and I have grown more and more in our trust in the Lord's care. We are growing in our faith and knowledge of Him." Mona paused just long enough for Ron to voice the remainder of the message.

"Everything we've shared with you can be backed up. The evidence is overwhelming for this plan of God as well as the relevance and reliability of Scripture." Ron stood up. "I want to give you something." He walked into the hallway. "I'll be right back." Mona and Suzanne looked at each other. Mona shrugged her shoulders; uncertain what Ron was going to give Suzanne.

Ron walked back into the room. "Before I give this to you, I want to caution you. If you begin to search for this evidence and answers from God with the intent that He must prove Himself to you, you may never truly receive the answers you seek. I realize that sounds strange."

Mona knew what Ron was getting at. "I think what Ron is saying is that everyone must first humble themselves before God, knowing that He is the supreme Lord over all. If we tell God that He has to prove Himself to us, then we are trying to take the place of God, insisting He meets our criteria for belief. We are standing in judgment of Him rather than allowing Him to reveal Himself to us. The evidence simply validates and verifies what He has revealed to us in our hearts and from His Word, the Bible. It substantiates all He has shown us about who He is. Does that make sense?"

"I think so. But you keep talking about the heart. What do you mean by that?

Ron had a good illustration, and so he spoke up. "The heart is like our mission control center. I'm not speaking about the organ that pumps blood. This mission control center brings forth the true essence of who we are. In fact, I think that what we are discovering from the Thought Transmission project is that people are more than a factory of chemicals and electrical impulses. You, more than anyone, know just how complicated our minds are. But what the Bible states is that we are made up of mind, body, and soul. The soul, or perhaps we might say the heart, is what drives us in all we think and do. It defines us. We can either have a hard heart that rejects the Lord or a soft, open heart toward God and His leading."

Suzanne tried to see what Ron was hiding behind his back. "So, what is this you have for me, Ron?"

Ron revealed the book he held in his left hand. Picking up a pen from the table, he scribbled a short note inside the front cover. "Here, I want you to have this. It's yours to keep." He handed Suzanne the book and then sat back down. She read the title and author out loud: *The Case for Christ* by Lee Strobel. I know I've heard of him but not sure from where. Anyway, that is very thoughtful, Ron. Thank you."

"Mr. Strobel set out to investigate the evidence for the resurrection of Christ. He was an investigative journalist who researched many different sources but was actually trying to disprove or at least bring a reason to discredit the resurrection. You see, Lee Strobel was an atheist. He did not want to believe. He had to come to terms with the evidence he uncovered. He wrote down the story of his own search for truth in this book. Suzanne, if you honestly want to know the truth, let God reveal it to you. I believe you might find you have some things in common with Mr. Strobel. I am asking you to read and investigate for yourself. Just be sure you do so with a humble heart because since God is real and rules over all His creation, we owe Him our utmost homage and respect."

Suzanne stood up. Mona and Ron did the same. "I really should be getting on home," she said as she turned toward the foyer.

Mona indicated a desire to get together again soon. Suzanne turned to face Ron and Mona. "Yes, I would like that."

Ron added, "We never really talked much about the progress of Thought Transmission. As we proceed, I would like to hear from you about how you think things are going."

Suzanne thought for a moment. "I would also like to hear from you about our progress."

The trio walked toward the front door. Ron called out to the kids to come and tell their guest goodbye. Jeremy walked in first, uncertain whether to offer his hand or not. Trevor and Brenda followed close behind. "Wait," Trevor announced. He ran to the back door where he met Sheldon who was anxious to greet his new friend once more. Sheldon let out a howl as he scampered up to Suzanne who knelt down and stroked behind his floppy ears. "And it was so nice meeting you, Sheldon."

Ron spoke up before Suzanne walked out the door. "So, Dr. Myers . . ." Ron met Suzanne's smile. "What's next on the team's agenda?"

"We're moving forward with Simon's encephal-egg, as he calls it. But it will be a while before we get back into full swing." Ron acknowledged as everyone waved farewell.

Suzanne drove away, contemplating the evening's discussion, her head spinning.

CHAPTER 23

JUNE 11, 2030
GENEVA SCIENCE CONFERENCE

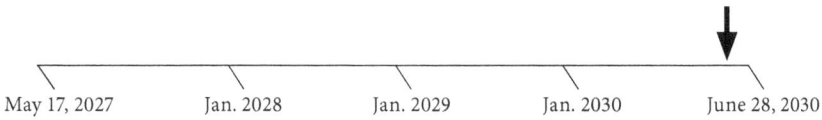

| May 17, 2027 | Jan. 2028 | Jan. 2029 | Jan. 2030 | June 28, 2030 |

D r. Suzanne Myers related the team's decision to move forward with Simon Loffler's idea to build a neuromorphic model of the brain. She decided to let Simon explain the next step along their journey. "And now our study and story became even more rewarding and, well, exciting. I'll let Simon Loffler provide you the simplified version of what happened next. Simon?"

Simon rose from his seat and sauntered over to the podium. He placed his notes in front of him and looked up at the audience and then back down again. He looked down at the slide presentation he would be using throughout his presentation. Looking up once more, he began his delivery. "A simplified version, Dr. Myers? Well, I'll try. Here goes. Neuromorphic engineering turned out to be the solution to our problem. I designed and created the skull cap we needed." An image of his skull cap was on the screens. "I have to say that no one until now has created a device of this magnitude, so I am very proud of this accomplishment." The crowd gave Simon an ovation, to which he gave a bow of appreciation. "We consulted my friend and colleague

Andreas Grisham who studied the math. He came up with an equation and utilized quantum field theory to accomplish our goal."

Simon looked up from his notes and saw an assortment of confused faces in the crowd. "All right, yeah. Like some of you, I don't know what all this means. I'm sure many of you, however, know your stuff in this field." Simon now wished he had studied the subject of quantum physics enough to come across as sounding more intelligent and knowledgeable. "Anyway, Andreas helped us build our model of the brain. We ended up calling it the encephal-egg, or just egg for short." Simon revealed a photo of the egg on the screens. "Andreas surmised we needed to utilize a crystallized gel solution along with what is called liquid scintillation to accomplish the task of successfully creating the egg that would mimic the human brain. Imbedded in the liquid crystal substance was a network of tiny wires made from pure silver—again, to mimic the neurotransmission pathways in the human brain itself. Inserting these tiny wires—several hundred, I might add—was painstakingly meticulous. This scintillation substance is made up of sodium iodide activated with a trace amount of thallium. Sandwiched between flexible translucent panes is a gas mixture of neon and xenon that, when stimulated, will emit red, green, or blue visible light. To put it simply, the neurotransmission pathways light up." Simon looked up from his notes and smiled. "It took quite a while to develop the egg. But I think you will see, along with our team, that it was all worth the effort." Simon half expected applause, but none came.

"And again, I want to recognize Andreas Grisham's contribution. He isn't here, but I want to thank him for all his . . ." The audience interrupted with a round of applause. "Heck, I'm not too proud to say it; I think the entire team deserves applause." The audience reacted with an even louder ovation. As they did so, Simon turned to face the team members sitting off to the side, directing the applause in their direction.

"Thank you," Simon continued. "I need to point out that we weren't out of the woods just yet. We found that we needed to increase the signal emanating from the transmitter's brain to obtain a proper reading. We added a rheostat to amplify the signal and then added a sound element to the transmission output. I have to tell you, the sound coming from the brain's neurotransmission was quite interesting. It was unlike anything I'd ever heard before. And yes, I actually have a recording. Check it out." Simon played a few seconds of the sound, which, to everyone's delight, was truly remarkable and unique. "Once the model was complete and connected to the computer, we needed to perform a trial run. Before connecting the transmission of thoughts from our transmitter over to a receiver of those thoughts, we needed to make sure we were receiving the appropriate data into our computer software." He looked down at his notes, hesitated, and then set them aside. His demeanor suddenly changed. Simon wanted to emphasize the turn of events at this juncture, so he looked up and stated emphatically, "Then something remarkable and unexpected occurred." Simon declared this last statement with enthusiasm. The crowd seemed to capture his excitement as all eyes were fixated on him. "Okay, I can see I've got you now. And I hate to disappoint you, but I'm not going to tell you the rest of the story." He then laughed. "I'm going to let Dr. Suzanne Myers take it from here." Suzanne walked to the podium. She caught Simon's eye and whispered to him "good job" as they crossed paths.

Dr. Myers placed her hands on both sides of the podium. She fixed her eyes on the audience sitting before her and scanned the room, making sure she had their attention before resuming her story. Simon had done well to create an aura of anticipation as all eyes were now transfixed on Suzanne.

"As Simon mentioned to you, a remarkable thing occurred on our first trial run with what we affectionately named the egg. An even more perplexing phenomenon occurred on our second trial run, which I will address sometime later. The first new phase of our experiments began with our volunteer associate Erin Roberts. You have heard me sing Erin's praises. She was unable to join us here today but has given us permission to disclose to you her own experience with this next step in the development of Thought Transmission. I believe we can all relate when I tell you that our experiments had their ups and downs. This portion of our journey, and even on the same day, contained an enormously low point, which was then balanced out by an enormous high point of discovery.

CHAPTER 24

DECEMBER 11, 2029
ROOM B11 OF THE NEUROSCIENCE BUILDING AT
KING'S UNIVERSITY-OVER ONE YEAR HAS PASSED
SINCE THE EGG'S INCEPTION

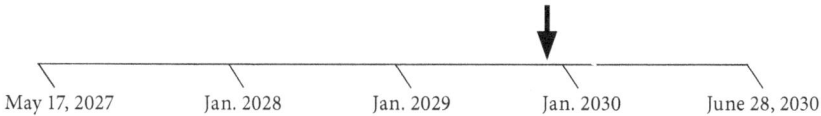

| May 17, 2027 | Jan. 2028 | Jan. 2029 | Jan. 2030 | June 28, 2030 |

A comfortable recliner sat empty in the basement room in the neuroscience wing at the university. On a wall behind the recliner was a two-way mirror. Simon's carefully constructed skull cap containing hundreds of tiny electrodes was in a corner of the room, having been forcibly flung there moments before. In the opposite corner on the floor sat Erin Roberts with arms encasing her knees pulled up to her chest. She was crying uncontrollably. The door to the room suddenly flew open as several members of the team hurried through the entrance.

"Erin, are you alright? What just happened?" Dr. Myers was perplexed as she tried to bring solace to this woman who only moments before had been jovial and excited about this new stage of discovery in thought transmission.

Erin lifted her head. "Why did you leave me in that dark place for so long?"

Suzanne knelt down alongside Erin. "Erin, the experiment only lasted a little over a minute before you . . ."

"No. How can you say that? It must have been hours. I know it was. It felt as though you all had abandoned me. I was finally able to throw off that awful cap and escape."

Simon, having entered the room, heard Erin's remark. "Yeah, about that skull cap . . ." His progression was immediately halted by Suzanne's stern look of disapproval.

"Erin, please tell us. What are you talking about?" Dr. Milton was trying to be sympathetic but knew they needed to gain a sense of what had taken place.

"You left me there for so long," she repeated. "It was just so dark and dismal . . . and lonely."

Randall Milton backed away as Suzanne and Nora tried to console Erin. A call on his cell phone caused him to step out of the room. "I have to take this. I'll be back in a moment."

Simon bent down to pick up the skull cap, looking for any damage that may have occurred. Andreas Grisham approached Simon. They began discussing the possible reasons for such an unexpected and shocking outcome.

Ron Provost had been invited to sit in on the experiment. He, too, was perplexed. "*What could have happened*?" he wondered. He noticed the puzzled look on the faces of both Simon and Andreas. "May I join you guys?"

"Absolutely." Simon waved Ron over. Andreas was just telling me about something unusual he noticed inside the egg—something he had never seen."

"That's right. This was not something that was supposed to happen. But I've seen this effect before."

"What do you mean?" asked Simon.

"Sometime back I was invited to the Sudbury Neutrino Observatory. I knew of their facility, but that was the first time I got to see what was happening up close. Are you both familiar with the SNO?"

"I've heard the name, but no, I don't know what it is," answered Simon.

Ron on the other hand was familiar with the facility and its purpose. "They study the effects of neutrinos."

"That's right." Andreas was about to explain what he had seen at the SNO when he was cut off by Simon's question. "What are neutrinos?" he asked.

Andreas swung into his nerd mode as he tried to explain. "They are tiny particles; I mean like the tiniest particle known to science, which is emitted from atomic reactions within the core of the Sun or other star and supernova formation and activity." Andreas was about to really pour on his typical science nerd lingo but decided to keep it simple. "And they travel near the speed of light. Nothing slows them down, and they can pass through anything in the known universe. And oh, by the way, they are thought to be the most abundant thing in the universe. Trillions pass through your body all the time." Simon was surprised that he had never heard of these neutrinos before. Andreas continued. "So anyway, this SNO facility is in the shape of a dome. It is filled with a liquid scintillator, the same stuff we have inside our encephal-egg. From time to time, a neutrino comes in contact with one of the atoms inside the scintillator. It causes a reaction, like a spark. It was this same kind of spark that I noticed inside the encephal-egg. Quite a few sparks, too, which is extremely rare."

"So, what are you suggesting?" Ron figured Andreas had some kind of explanation.

"Well, here's the thing. I noticed hundreds of sparks in the few seconds we opened up the neurotransmission line. Guys . . . that simply doesn't happen."

By now Erin was back on her feet. Her fear of "that dark place" was subsiding and was now replaced by embarrassment and humiliation. Erin prided herself in her own self-sufficiency and ability to remain in control. She would have preferred to come through this ordeal with the confident assurance of "Invictus"— "I am the master of my fate. I am the captain of my soul." This was not to be the case. This episode along with the occurrence on the Silhouette Trail and other events over the past several months brought such personal caliber into question. She was coming to the realization that she may not be as strong and in control of her faculties as she thought. She turned to face Dr. Myers as together they made their way to the door. Making sure everyone in the room could hear, Erin proclaimed, "I never want to undergo that, ever again." Everyone gave her a look of empathy.

The three men continued discussing the anomalies of the morning's event. "What do you mean by 'this simply doesn't happen'?" Ron realized that Andreas must be onto something.

"I mean that the neutrino reaction within the scintillation rarely occurs."

Simon pointed out another observation. "Once we opened up the neurotransmission line to the egg, we allowed one minute to pass before I amplified the signal. Andreas, was that when you first noticed the sparks?"

"Yes, I think so."

"Okay. Something else occurred." Simon needed to share his own observations. "As you know, we added a sound element along with the visual on the monitor. Both suddenly flatlined."

"What do you mean they flatlined?" asked Ron.

"I mean that that the visual readout of brain activity went from the typical sine wave activity to flatline. And the sound was a constant tone . . . or at least at first."

"Yes, go on." Andreas implored Simon to continue.

"Well, only after about three seconds, the flatline seemed to encounter a wall. The visual went berserk for a moment, and the sound had a screeching sound to it, but then they both flatlined once again only to do the same thing again after another few seconds."

"How long did this anomaly occur?" Andreas asked the question, but Ron was also curious.

"No more than about 15 seconds. That's when Erin threw off the skull cap and lept from the chair."

"And to her, it felt like hours," Ron recalled what Erin had said. "Let's get back to the neutrino factor. Andreas, is it possible that these neutrinos could have traveled down the silver wires back into Erin's brain?"

"Like I said, nothing whatsoever either attracts neutrinos or causes them to veer off their usual light-speed course."

"Until now," Ron declared emphatically. Simon and Andreas looked at one another and then back to Ron.

"We're talking about something that defies physical science." Andreas' training wouldn't allow him to consider anything that fell outside the bounds of physics.

By this time, Suzanne, Nora, and Randall had returned to the room. Erin was still shaken, so they had sent her home.

"Have you come up with some sort of explanation?" asked Dr. Milton.

Andreas and Simon shared their own observations with the team. Although they had no explanation, they did perceive that the increase in the amplitude of the signal was what brought on the effects inside Erin's mind. Meanwhile, Ron was caught up in his own theory related to the neutrino effect. While Andreas and Simon both could find no logical or scientific reason to explain what took place, Ron was theorizing an alternative possibility. "*Could it be that neutrinos are attracted to human thought?*" He knew that his hypothesis defied known scientific principles, so kept his speculation to himself. He then thought about the matter pertaining to Erin's perspective on time. The actual time Erin first began experiencing the "dark place" until she threw off the skull cap was around 15 seconds. But she said it felt like hours. In Ron's Christian perspective, the only place where linear time might not exist is in eternity. "Impossible," Ron whispered to himself. "*There has to be another explanation. We need to find the answer.*"

Without giving it a second thought, Ron interrupted the team's conversation and exclaimed, "Let's run it again!"

All eyes and ears suddenly turned toward Ron. "What? Did you say run it again?" asked Dr. Myers.

"Yes. Hook me up. We can run it again but with a few changes."

Dr. Myers immediately halted Ron from saying anything further. "I'm sorry, Ron, but we'll do nothing of the sort. Where on earth are you coming from by making such a suggestion? No, wait! I don't even want to know. The answer is an emphatic no!"

"Look, Dr. Myers, we've only got about six months until the Geneva Conference. We need to find some answers . . . and I have a theory."

Nora spoke up. "He's got a point, Suzanne. If Ron has a theory, then maybe we should run with it."

Dr. Milton agreed with Nora. Andreas, too, was on board.

Ron's adrenaline was in high gear. "You're going to just have to trust me. Simon, can we do this? Is the cap still okay?"

"It's fine. But Ron, you are going to have to give us something to work with here. We don't want to have to pick up the pieces of your shattered emotions like we did with Erin."

"I realize I might experience the same thing, Simon, but I'm going to suggest some changes. First, let's not immediately amplify the neurotransmission signals to the same level as before. Allow the line to be open for a few minutes, long enough to see if you are getting the readings you need. Then raise the amplitude incrementally. Make a note of the time and the readings with each step. Once you reach the same intensity level you had with Erin, leave the transmission line open for no more than 10 seconds. See if you get the same readings as before. Like Erin, I'll have my consistent thought, which I'll repeat over and over in my mind."

"And we'll see if we experience the same neutrino effect," added Andreas.

"I can see I'm in the minority," admitted Suzanne. "All right, everyone. Nora, I'll need you to be our timekeeper. Simon, you just focus on the transmission lines and incremental steps in amplitude. Let's go with six incremental steps. Andreas, please watch the activity inside the egg . . . and take notes. Dr. Milton and I will watch the brain activity on the monitor. And I'm curious about that strange sound element we experienced with Erin. And, oh, Simon, please make sure you record all the data."

"That goes without saying, Dr. Myers," Simon replied.

Ron made a phone call to his wife, Mona, before releasing his phone to the team. He requested that she join them at the facility. She agreed to be there within 20 minutes.

Ron considered the thought he would concentrate on and repeat throughout the experiment. He thought of the words from Isaiah 26:3— "The steadfast of mind You will keep in perfect peace, because he trusts in You."

JANUARY 13, 2030
RON AND MONA ENJOY AN EVENING OF CONVERSATION WITH DR. SUZANNE MYERS AT THE PROVOST HOME

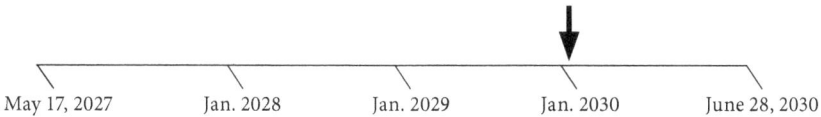

| May 17, 2027 | Jan. 2028 | Jan. 2029 | Jan. 2030 | June 28, 2030 |

"Come in out of the cold, Suzanne." Mona ushered Suzanne into the foyer. "I can't believe you decided to accept our invitation in this weather. I didn't realize the wind would become so fierce."

"I can usually stand the cold. It's that windchill that makes it so miserable." Suzanne took off her coat and hat and handed them to Mona, who hung them in the entry closet.

Ron walked into the room. "Hey! We're honored you decided to join us this cold Sunday afternoon."

"Suzanne was mentioning the windchill. What is it today, Ron?"

"I think it's in the minus 20s today. Just be glad we're not in Montreal. Low minus 30s there, I think."

"Let's get you warmed up. We have a good fire going." Mona walked ahead into the living room. Ron followed behind and offered Suzanne a seat near the fireplace.

Suzanne sat down and reached out to warm her hands. "I'm glad you invited me. Actually, I was thinking of inviting you two, but you beat me to the punch. Ron, you and I haven't had a chance to talk since our last test. I'm curious about getting your feedback on what happened that day." Suzanne detected an obvious lack of noise in the house. "Oh, where are the kids? And Sheldon?"

"They are over at my sister's house," Mona advised. "Sheldon too."

Ron leaned over in his chair, elbows resting on his legs. "Well, that's one of the reasons we invited you over. I want to get your take on that day as well."

Suzanne took out a pad of paper containing a few notes and questions. "Andreas mentioned seeing a strange phenomenon take place inside the egg. He said he thought it was neutrinos colliding with atoms inside the scintillation substance. He then noticed a great deal more radiance coming from the transmission lines. My question is this: What did this have to do with either your or Erin's experience, if any?"

"I've thought about it a lot. I don't think you are going to like what I have to say." Ron sat back in his chair.

"Oh? Why is that?"

"Because my theory does not line up with accepted scientific facts. Believe me when I say that I'm not given to weird paranormal occurrences or alien abductions and things such as these. I believe almost everything can be explained by known laws within the universe. But I also know that things happen that cannot be fully explained by known science. I would like to ask you first. What do you think happened?"

Suzanne shook her head. "The team hasn't come up with answers. We tried to explain the brain scan and strange wave activity. We have never witnessed this kind of response to brain activity. We found no way to explain the activity inside the egg. Then the biggest puzzle of all is why you apparently experienced a sense of euphoria, but Erin described it as dreadful. Ron, you still haven't fully told us what you experienced. Why?"

"I'm still coming to grips with that. I can't find the right words to explain the occurrence."

Mona added, "Ron hasn't even given me the full experience."

Ron took a Bible from off the side table and held it up. "The Bible relates encounters that various individuals had with heavenly visions. Daniel, Ezekiel, Paul, and John found it difficult to put into words what they encountered. At times they had to use earthly terms to try to explain what they could not truly conceive or describe. In a way, that's what I'm having trouble coming up with. Although with me, it was more of a wondrous sensation than a vision. I did, however, see things that are too marvelous to describe."

"Ron, you said you had a theory as to what occurred. I promise to keep an open mind."

"All right. As I mentioned, I believe I had an encounter with things not of this world. Erin, too, I think. First of all, yes, I believe neutrinos played a part in what took place. I believe that because they are the smallest known particle in the universe, they actually skimmed the surface of eternity and then relayed whatever they retained back to my mind and Erin's." Ron paused to gain a sense of Suzanne's reaction.

Suzanne had been leaning in toward the fire but suddenly sat back. "Oh my!" was all she could find to say.

"Think of it this way. If we were able to zoom in to the microscopic world past the smallest substance in the void of space, what would we find? A void of nothing at all? A barrier? What? I believe what we eventually come to is eternity itself. This eternal realm has no beginning, and it has no end. Linear time ceases to exist. Eternity simply is. I believe that since neutrinos are the smallest particle, they actually skim the surface of this eternal realm—the realm of God."

Suzanne turned to Mona. "Has he related this to you?"

"Only some of it. Keep listening." Mona was intent on Ron keeping Suzanne's attention.

Ron glared for a moment at the crackling blaze of the fire. He had always been captivated by flickering flames. He then focused his attention once more on Suzanne. "Now I'm going to mention something that might sound arrogant and perhaps a bit insensitive. I do not mean to come off that way, but I have to mention this. First, I believe those neutrinos are actually attracted to the mind, and even the soul, of people. I think it goes even farther than that. If they actually skim eternity and retain the essence of the divine, then perhaps they are attracted to one of the only sources of that same realm on Earth—the heart of humankind—of some, anyway."

"Ron, you can't be serious. That's ridiculous."

Mona turned to face Suzanne. "Wait, Suzanne. Hear him out. Please."

Ron continued. "The Bible declares that when a person places his or her trust in Christ rather than themselves for rescue from bondage to sin within and the outward influence of a corrupt world, a wonderful thing happens. The Spirit of God comes to live within the heart, or soul, of that individual. In other words, God knows we are hopeless sinners apart from His intervention. We try to overcome the struggles and temptations we face by convincing ourselves that the answers come from within our own ability to deal with them. They don't. We are powerless to save ourselves. God does not change us from the outside in through religious rituals and trying to work really hard to overcome sin and do what is right. Laws and rules do little to change the heart of an individual. Psychological therapy only changes behavior but does little to change the heart. Even emotional highs during a worship service are of no value in countering sin's effects on each of us. Instead, He changes us from the inside out. The Spirit of God comes to live within the heart of believers and puts them on a path from a self-oriented life to a Christ-oriented life. And Suzanne, I'm not making this up. Scripture makes this clear."

Suzanne was showing signs of agitation. "Ron. Ron! You can talk all day long about what's in the Bible, but what does this have to do with what happened to you and Erin?"

Mona reached over and took Suzanne's hand. Suzanne's instinct was to snatch her hand away, but she decided against it. She did not acknowledge Mona's display of affection. Mona could sense Suzanne's discomfort and lifted her hand from Suzanne's.

"I know all this sounds ridiculous," Ron continued. "I'm going to ask you to listen with the attitude of scientific discovery. Listen to the evidence and try not to immediately discredit what I say."

"That's fine. I'm sorry for my outburst. I said I would listen with an open mind. You said you have given this much thought. I want you to know, Ron, that I respect you as a fellow scientist. So . . . please . . . continue."

"If I am right about neutrinos being attracted to the human soul, the only creation made in the image of God as the book of Genesis points out, then here's my explanation of why Erin and I had a different experience while encountering neutrinos. First, I need to point out that these experiences did not occur until Simon amplified the signal. That may have been the catalyst to divert the neutrinos from their normal course and travel through the transmission lines to our minds. In my case, I have God's Spirit living within me, as I mentioned before. I believe I had a positive encounter with the eternal realm of God, which the neutrinos had absorbed. I know from speaking with Erin that she has never placed her trust and hope in the saving work and person of Jesus Christ. And because of that, the divine essence picked up by neutrinos was repelled by Erin's rejection of God's Spirit. She had a negative encounter. While I experienced joy and peace from this heavenly realm of God, she did not. She experienced despair."

Ron felt he needed to wrap up his analysis, for now, giving Suzanne some time to process what he just said.

Suzanne placed her notebook on the coffee table. She first looked at Mona and then at Ron. "Ron, you know I come from a naturalistic perspective in how I view our world, especially the condition of all people. Every cause in the universe comes from within the universe, not from a supernatural cause outside of time and matter. The things you've told me, fly in the face of everything I believe. To accept this explanation means I have to change my entire worldview."

Mona spoke up. "We realize this is hard to swallow. Ron debated whether to even mention these things to you. But he felt he needed to be honest with you. There is a lot at stake."

"And I will admit," added Ron, "that part of my account contains elements from my Christian worldview. But I have weighed them against the facts and evidence. As you mentioned, the team has no scientific basis on which to make sense of it all." Ron lifted his finger to indicate he had more to say. "So what I am asking you to do is to think very carefully and seriously about what I have shared with you."

Mona felt led to mention another aspect of the conversation. "I know we talked on the topic of God, Jesus, the Holy Spirit, the Bible, and heaven this afternoon as well as the last time we met. We shared what is called in the New Testament the gospel. Do you recall?"

"Yes. I haven't read the book you gave me, but I'm thinking about it. Please understand that I'm the type of person who finds it hard to accept things without the benefit of evidence. You implied that Mr. Strobel's book presents evidence for the resurrection of Jesus, among other aspects of the Christian faith. I may read it and will give some consideration to all you have told me. But please don't push me too much."

Ron and Mona were pleased that Suzanne was giving the Christian message some consideration but needed to give her a warning. Ron looked at Mona, who knew what he was thinking.

"Suzanne, the evidence for Jesus as the Son of God, the message of rescue from sin, of forgiveness, and of new life, along with the reliability of the Scriptures, are there for all to explore. They confirm the truth we shared. Let's face it. Even creation itself gives evidence for the existence and character of God. But we need to give you a warning. We mentioned this the last time we met, but I want to emphasize it again."

"You cautioned me not to judge God."

"Yes. In our search for evidence of God, Christ, and the reliability of Scripture, we might find ourselves placing God under a microscope. That relegates God to a place of dishonor. We are, in essence, trying to unseat His rightful position and throne."

"I tried to do just that, Suzanne, many years ago," Mona pointed out. "I believed in God but I had doubts too. I started searching for the truth. I found the truth but failed to find God."

"What do you mean?" Suzanne asked.

"As Ron mentioned, the truth will prevail in our search for answers, but even then we may have missed God. In my case, I had no peace in my life. I had not approached Him humbly but prided myself in discovering the truth. That did little to change my life. The reason is that I was still trying to be the one in control. I had not let go of my own life. I did not face the fact that I needed to give Jesus, my Lord, control of my life. Jesus said that if someone wants to save their own life, they will lose it. 'But whoever loses his life for My sake will find it' (Matt. 16:25). He said that after telling His disciples that if they wanted to be His followers, they would have to take up their cross and follow Him. And that is where true faith comes in. We place our life in His hands—no matter what."

"There's something else I want to mention." Ron sensed that Suzanne was troubled by what she was hearing. He saw this as a good sign. "I want to tell you that as you start to give consideration to this offer of love and mercy being extended to you through our Lord's redemption, you might begin to feel uneasy. You will begin to feel convicted about sins in your life. That's okay. It means the Holy Spirit is drawing you to the Lord. God is inclining your heart toward Him, even as you start your search. The sad fact is that no one truly seeks for God without God's intervention. Our nature of rebellion resists a desire to know God. The Bible, in the third chapter of the book of Romans, repeats what Psalm 53 says about this—that no one seeks for God, not one. "

"And please, Suzanne, don't resist Him," Mona added. "Yes, go ahead and look into the evidence, but just realize that head knowledge never saved anyone. The Lord needs to enter your heart. And don't extend an invitation to Him to 'come into your heart,' as many like to say. Instead, receive the invitation He is making to you to receive His salvation and presence within your heart."

Suzanne stood up as if intending to leave. "Ron, Mona, I just need to ask. Where is this God, especially when heartache and pain show up in life?"

Ron had the answer. "He is as close as a prayer, whether voiced or even as intimate as a thought."

A conflict began to stir in Suzanne's mind and heart. "I'll keep that in mind . . . and yes, that pun was intended."

The mood suddenly changed as all three began to laugh. Ron opened the door, and they stepped out onto the front porch. The wind had died down somewhat but was still blowing, although they could not tell from which direction it came or where it was headed.

CHAPTER 26

JUNE 11, 2030
GENEVA CONFERENCE RON RELATES HIS EXPERIENCE WITH NEUTRINOS

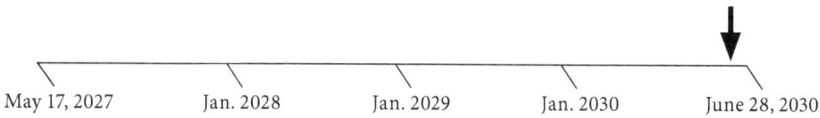

| May 17, 2027 | Jan. 2028 | Jan. 2029 | Jan. 2030 | June 28, 2030 |

Suzanne told about the team's trial run using the egg. She told of Erin Roberts' wretched experience and how perplexed they all were about what caused Erin such anguish. This brought Suzanne's remarks to the point of Ron Provost's insistence that they run the test again, using himself as the test subject.

Suzanne checked the time. "At this point, we are giving you a 15-minute recess. When you return, Ron Provost will relate his own remarkable experience with the egg as well as those mysterious particles known as neutrinos. His story will surely keep you on edge, so please be sure to be in your seats shortly after the notice to return. And as a reminder, this afternoon's session led by Dr. Randal Milton will feature two other volunteers, Kiara Patel and Anthony Schumacher. They will describe the success we have experienced over the past few months with more advanced levels of thought."

Suzanne walked back to where members of the team were seated. Together they all walked out to the lobby for a break. Ron, however, remained seated. His wife, Mona, was seated on the front row and observed Ron deep in thought. She was with Ron that day he underwent the test run with the egg. Afterward, he was quiet and reserved and had a presence of peace about him. Later, Ron began to open up to Mona about his experience but did not fully comprehend his venture or how to describe the feeling. He said it was as if he had become immersed in God's love. Ron had admitted to Mona that he was uncertain of what to say or divulge to the crowd this day. Mona sensed that was keeping Ron deep in thought at this moment. She finally walked up to the edge of the stage and caught his attention. He smiled at her.

"Are you apprehensive, Ron?" she asked.

"Not apprehensive, no. I just realize there are some things I can share about my experience, but there are also some things I shouldn't mention. I'll explain later, Sweetheart."

Mona just nodded. "I trust you will know what to say and what not to say when the time comes. I'm confident the Lord will guide your speech."

Ron took a deep breath, smiled, and nodded back at this woman God had graciously placed in his life.

"Can I get you some water?" Mona asked.

"That's okay. I'm coming down." He and Mona walked out to the lobby. Several attendees walked up to him, shook his hand, and gave him words of encouragement and appreciation.

≈≈≈≈

The attendees began making their way back to their seats as Suzanne turned the microphone back over to Ron Provost who continued relating his experience.

"Once Simon placed the skull cap on my head, everyone except Nora left the room and entered the control room. That basement room does a great job of keeping out extraneous noise. It was quiet and warm despite the low temps outside on this mid-January day. Despite what Erin had just gone through, I felt confident that the changes we implemented would provide the results the team needed. I closed my eyes, repeating over and over the thought in my head. Several minutes passed as Simon began to increase the amplitude in the transmission lines. At some point, I lost consciousness, at least a conscious awareness of my external surroundings. Simon and other members of the team later told me that an unexplained phenomenon occurred on my brain scan monitor. They were all alarmed when every phase of the readout from the egg flatlined. They were about to disconnect me when the monitor scan began to move once more but in a manner no one had ever witnessed before. Rather than the usual sharp up and down wave movements that are typical of brain activity, the monitor showed several waves crisscrossing simultaneously as if indicating a musical score. Not only that, but Simon had raised the sound volume they had implemented coming from the egg. Simon was recording all of this, which I was later able to see and hear for myself. The sound was unrecognizable. Let me put it this way: How might you describe to a deaf person who has never heard sound before, the sound of birds or animals? They would have no concept. In the same way, none of us on the team can compare the sound coming from my brain to any known source. It was completely unique."

The sound technician began playing the unusual sound the team had heard that day. Every person seated in the auditorium was mesmerized by something they had never heard before. Ron continued. "On top of all that, Andreas was watching the encephal-egg and taking notes of what he saw. He noticed sparks emitting inside the egg, just as he had seen when Erin underwent her trial run. But this time, the transmission lines began to light up with a blend of colors. Andreas told me later that it was a beautiful sight. He couldn't take his eyes off of it." The audience was given the opportunity to witness this same scene. A sense of serenity and wonder filled the crowd. "And then there's this: All of the team could see my face. They said I was grinning ear to ear."

Ron paused to regain his focus. "So that portion of my story I have retold from what others related to me. Let me now give you the rest of the story."

Ron had thought many times since his encounter that day with neutrinos about what he would say to this crowd. He had debated whether to relate the fullness of that experience or just share a few minor details. The experience was deeply personal and intimate. As such he was not comfortable relating such matters in a public setting like this. Even as he stood before this crowd, he was unsure what words would emerge from his lips.

Ron hesitated to speak. A delay of a few seconds turned into a full minute. Suzanne, who sat over to the side of the stage with others on the team, was becoming unsettled. She looked at Nora who then looked at Dr. Engel sitting off stage. He, too, was perplexed and shrugged. Suzanne decided she needed to intervene, so she stood, intending to walk over to Ron. As she did so, Ron suddenly opened his mouth.

"Folks, how do I describe an event that, to my knowledge, no one else has ever experienced?" Ron lingered for several more seconds. "After giving it much thought, I have decided not to try to explain this experience on a personal level." The audience gave a disappointing response. "If I use a scientific explanation to describe what took place, I would only be speculating. I would like, however, to propose what I believe occurred that day from a somewhat pseudo-scientific perspective. But to do so requires me to go beyond a strictly naturalistic viewpoint. Dr. Myers and I have discussed my summations, but I cannot attest to whether she or any other team member would accept what I am about to tell you. My hope and prayer are that you will receive what I tell you with an open mind." An unsettled audience response was quickly replaced with silent anticipation.

"On a personal level, I will simply tell you that what I experienced was serene and pleasant. Now here is my speculative account as to what occurred." Ron glanced at the scribbled notes he had written earlier and then tucked them into his shirt pocket. "As Simon related to you, neutrinos are the smallest known particle in the entire universe. They skim through space, moving even past the smallest atoms and other microscopic particles. There is no mass we know of that can hinder their course. They continue their journey through the universe with nothing to impede or thwart their progress. They have little detectable mass. Science has yet to discover an energy source other than the atomic reaction that brought about their initial creation and propulsion. But I have another theory."

Ron glanced toward the team. He was surprised to see Suzanne's face displaying an agreeable smile. She and Nora both displayed a hint of approval of where they anticipated Ron's theory would lead. Ron then looked down at Mona on the front row. She mouthed "I love you" when she saw him look her way. It was her love that often motivated him through his pursuits.

Ron had prayed silently before addressing this crowd, knowing he would be crossing some barriers in the minds of some. "Beyond the smallest particle in space, beyond even neutrinos themselves, is another realm. I believe it to be the eternal realm—the area that exists beyond the boundary of matter and time. God's domain." Ron could hear stirring among his audience. He did not let that deter him. "I believe neutrinos skim this eternal realm of God. Although they do not exist in this eternal realm, I believe that to be their source of energy. I can compare it to phytoplankton, microscopic organisms floating on the surface of the ocean yet they receive their energy from the Sun. Take them from the sea, and they cease to exist. Not only do neutrinos obtain energy from this eternal realm, but I will go so far as to suggest that they reflect or absorb a portion of this eternal domain." Ron paused briefly. "They retain the domain of God." The murmuring in the crowd now became more intense. Ron knew he was losing many in the audience with this talk of the eternal realm of God and that he needed to provide the evidence for such bold conjecture.

"I believe there is only one element in our universe that attracts neutrinos. I believe it to be the mind . . . and perhaps even the human soul." From this declaration, many in the audience voiced their displeasure. One person yelled, "I thought this was a science conference, not a church revival!" A smattering of applause came from another area of the crowd. Murmuring continued throughout the auditorium.

Dr. Milton leaned toward Dr. Myers. "You've got to stop this, Suzanne." Without facing Randall, she simply shook her head while raising her palm to Dr. Milton. He continued to stare at Suzanne in disgust.

Ron raised his voice above the dissenting voices. "I realize I have touched a nerve and gone beyond known scientific hypothesis. But hear me out." The noise level softened enough that Ron felt he could proceed. "What I experienced was unlike anything I have ever experienced within my body, mind, or emotions. I do not want to share too much for reasons I won't go into at this time. What I believe happened was that when Simon and the team began to raise the amplification of neurotransmissions in the egg, it became a kind of a magnet for the neutrinos. They followed the path of transmission lines into my brain. My brain reacted to what the neutrinos had absorbed from skimming eternity. I used the term *soul* because this was not just something that entered my mind but seemed to emanate throughout my very being."

Ron had tried to be careful with his words while relaying the message he wanted these renowned scientists and educators to hear. Some in the crowd were voicing their displeasure, while others issued forth words of encouragement.

Ron leaned into the microphone to be sure all could hear above the clamor. "Thank you for the opportunity to share my interpretation of what I believe took place with my encounter, as well as Erin Roberts' encounter with neutrinos." With that, he turned and walked back to his seat with the team.

Suzanne slowly stood and walked to the microphone. The audience was still in an uproar. She waited for the noise level to subside and then spoke. "From a naturalistic point of view, there is no easy answer for what took place that day. As a scientist, I will continue to explore the marvels of the universe. As a fellow human being, I will listen and learn and then try to make sense of revelation that comes my way." The clamor from the audience finally ceased. "I want to thank you all for being with us today. I also want to thank our team members for their dedication and contributions to our study of Thought Transmission. We will continue to explore the wonders of the human mind as we find additional ways to communicate the thoughts and intentions of one human mind and soul to another. I encourage you all to return this afternoon to hear what Dr. Milton and our two volunteers have to say. They will relate to you what

I believe is the true essence of why we began this study in the first place. You will then learn how adjustments were made utilizing the encephal-egg, which allowed us to transmit complex thoughts and even emotions from one mind and soul of an individual to another. He will relate the benefits our project will bring to the neurological and medical world, as well as the entire scientific community. It is certainly our honor to present our findings to you, our esteemed colleagues. I will now turn the microphone back over to Dr. Hermann Engel who will dismiss you."

Dr. Suzanne Myers sat back down as Dr. Engel emerged from behind the side corridor. He walked to the center of the stage. The only sound was clicking from the soles of his shoes crossing the stage floor. The crowd stared at him, wondering what he might add to the presentations delivered to them that day. Dr. Engel glanced across the crowd and then back to the esteemed neuroscientist and her team. "What more can I add?" He bowed his head briefly and then looked up. "My fellow associates, we must not discount the findings of scientific discovery, no matter how much it might infringe on our own views." He paused briefly, gathered his thoughts, and then added, "I believe we must concede the observation made by Yuval Noah Harari, the famous Israeli historian and a tenured professor in the Department of History at the Hebrew University of Jerusalem, who made his now famous statement, 'The greatest scientific discovery was the discovery of ignorance. Once humans realized how little they knew about the world, they suddenly had very good reason to seek new knowledge, which opened up the scientific road to progress.'"[1]

With that, Dr. Engel dismissed the crowd. Many remained as they shared anxious thoughts with one another before heeding his invitation to clear the auditorium.

CHAPTER 27

JUNE 11, 2030
IT IS THE MORNING OF SUZANNE MYERS' PRESENTATION TO THE SCIENCE SYMPOSIUM SHE IS INSIDE HER HOTEL ROOM MOMENTS BEFORE MAKING HER WAY TO THE GENEVA CONFERENCE CENTER

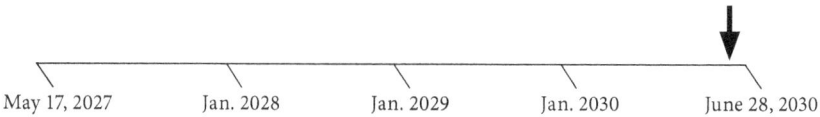

May 17, 2027   Jan. 2028   Jan. 2029   Jan. 2030   June 28, 2030

Suzanne Myers sat looking at her laptop screen. She had been awake for a good portion of the night in research. Ponderings that had occupied sleepless nights months before had been replaced by another curious priority. The Thought Transmission and neutrino study that had held her captive for so long was coming to an end, and not so much an end but the launching pad to even greater research and application. The course of this study had played a small part in opening the door to a newfound curiosity that had begun several weeks back. She reflected on the compatibility factor between transmitter and receiver. Thoughts alone were not the only entity being transferred. Emotions and even the very soul were perhaps being transferred from one individual to another. Why had common religious convictions been a factor in successful transmissions? Why did these same convictions regarding God make such a difference in the neutrino study? Or did they? She turned her attention to the discussions with Ron and Mona Provost. These talks had prompted attempts by her to discredit their assertions concerning the Christian message. She was now plagued and enraptured by the mounting evidence affirming those claims. Now she sat in the quiet of her hotel room as the morning sun streamed through the open curtain. She was coming to various conclusions regarding this subject that had so entangled her mind and emotions. Tears began to form.

"God, how can You be real? Everything in me wants to deny You, but the evidence simply won't allow it." She placed her hand on an open Bible. "And then there's the matter of this book." The claim that God was the author was preposterous, or so she had maintained. She now doubted her first assumptions.

Suzanne studied every angle. She examined the historical evidence verifying the Bible's veracity. Secular writers who tried to find fault with the Christian message ended up testifying to the accuracy of the biblical account. Archaeology confirmed many of the related events and places in Scripture. As to the Scriptures themselves, she first began to examine the chain of custody of the New Testament Scriptures from the earliest manuscripts up through the early church fathers. The writings had been copied meticulously and handed down through subsequent generations from three separate parts of the world, and yet the consistency of the manuscripts and books used were found to be the same. She found that the New Testament edition she referenced had been translated from the earliest Greek texts. These early texts had undergone the science of textual criticism and were found to be consistent. The minor textual errors had been compared with over 25,000 ancient Greek, Coptic, Latin, and other transcripts that were used to determine the actual words transcribed from the original manuscripts. Even minor variations had not changed the intended message. She turned her attention to the Old Testament and found the message weaved a consistent theme throughout the first words of Genesis to its fulfillment in the New Testament.

She had a few discussions with Ron and Mona Provost who emphasized what they called the gospel of Jesus Christ. The Apostle Paul and other New Testament writers continually referenced this gospel of Christ in their writings. She had turned a deaf ear to the message that God had been born a man at a specified time and place in history. This Son of God had come to provide a means to restore humanity to God the Father. Suzanne remained unconvinced that this Jesus was actually God in human form or that His death had solved any dilemma of sin. The outward evidence and the inward revelation were steering her in a new direction, but she still retained her doubts.

"I'm a scientist," she continually declared to Ron and Mona. "I cannot accept anything based on blind faith."

Ron Provost insisted that the gospel and the biblical accounts were never intended to be received in blind faith. The evidence was there to back up the claims of Christ and the words of Scripture. There was nothing blind about faith. Ron and Mona urged her to continue to examine the evidence even though they had said the evidence was not what would save her. "Why do you keep saying I need to be saved? Saved from what?" They tried to explain, but she continually turned away any notion that she needed to change to suit this God of theirs.

And then there was the matter of the book Ron had given her. She looked at the title, *The Case for Christ*, by Lee Strobel. "The author was where you are now," Ron told her. "Mr. Strobel didn't want to believe, so he began his own research. Anyway, I thought you might find it helpful."

"That is very thoughtful, Ron. Thank you." She was actually taken aback a bit by his boldness. She felt judged—again—to a degree but was at a point where she had to agree that the book might be a good resource.

She had begun to read the book several weeks back. It was Mr. Strobel's own journey of discovery that had prompted the impetus for Suzanne to spend this night reviewing the prophetic text of the Old Testament concerning the coming Messiah. For it was the New Testament writers who claimed that numerous prophecies had been fulfilled in this One who had been born into the world, performed miracles of healing and power over nature, taught the people, claimed to be one with God, rebuked the religious elite, was crucified for His claim of deity but was then raised to life. Suzanne would not immediately accept the writers' claims that Jesus had risen from the dead. She examined every possible explanation by skeptics to counter a risen Jesus. She found no merit in any of these accounts. The historic record of the resurrection and the vain attempts by others to discredit it would not allow her to deny the claim.

She eventually turned her attention to the internal evidence of Scripture itself. Matthew's Gospel said in the 28th verse of the 20th chapter that Jesus had come to "give His life as a ransom for many." She noticed in the footnotes a reference to the 53rd chapter of Isaiah; "My Servant, will justify the many, for He will bear their wrongdoings" and that He "bore the sin of many, and interceded for the wrongdoers." She checked the time period of this writing verified by the historic record. It was written some 700 years before the birth of Jesus. She was immediately taken by the way this prophet of old had so accurately portrayed the death and the apparent purpose of this interceder, Jesus. "The first-century believers must have doctored the text," she thought. She discovered that the Hebrew Bible, even in today's translation, contains these same words. The Hebrew Bible came from the Septuagint, a Greek translation from the ancient Hebrew and Aramaic developed sometime within 200 to 300 years before the birth of Jesus. The 53rd chapter of Isaiah had not been doctored or altered.

It had taken her all night to examine the prophetic evidence found in the Old Testament Scriptures. She had become weary and would have turned off her computer but for one verse that suddenly appeared on her screen. She read it to herself out loud. "And you will seek Me and find Me when you search for Me with all your heart." This was from Jeremiah 29:13.

She remembered the words Mona Provost had said to her. "Suzanne, we realize you are searching for the truth. We will pray that our Lord reveals Himself to your heart. Until that happens, all your searching will only result in further confusion and lack of peace." Ron then added, "And once God makes Himself known to you, all this research will flood your mind and heart and affirm what God Himself reveals to your heart. You will find peace when that happens."

Now, as Suzanne read this verse from the Prophet Jeremiah, in an instant, much of these findings came together in her mind. The Provosts' predictive words were coming true. Awareness came to Suzanne as she realized just how hard her own heart had become. "All my heart?" She had to laugh knowing that this recent search had not at all been for the purpose of seeking God. She had been stiff-arming this One who had pursued her and brought her to this point of recognizing her own rebellious heart. And sin. Yes, she would call it what it was—sin. Her heart was now broken as she read once more the account of Jesus's crucifixion and suffering. She realized that He had, indeed, paid an awful price for *her* sin and rebellion. She read the passage in Jeremiah once more. "And you will seek Me and find Me when you search for Me with all your heart." "Those words were meant for *me*," she whispered to herself. In an instant, peace replaced the turmoil that had been brewing in her heart.

In tears, she found herself falling to her knees. With her head bowed, she tried to form the words she needed to speak to this relentless pursuer of her soul. "God, I haven't spoken to you since I was maybe seven years old. So, I'm a little out of practice." She chuckled quietly to herself. "You simply won't let me go, will You? Well, here I am, the one who keeps pushing You away." She paused and then looked up. "Okay. You win. I've had You under a microscope, and it was wrong to judge You. I see that now. You are the rightful Judge. I'm guilty of rejecting You over and over again." She continued to try to find the words to speak to this once elusive concept that had now become the One who was waiting patiently at the door of her heart. "So, God, let's get real—You and me. You apparently know my thoughts. You know my heart. Oh, God, I've been wondering. Should we continue to go on with this research?" Suzanne had begun to doubt the validity of all this time and study over the past two years. "We've even attempted to skim Your eternal domain. And now You are inviting me to that same eternal home. Thank You for opening my eyes, loving me, and forgiving me for rejecting You for so long. What a fool I've been. So now what, Lord? I have to go talk to this crowd. What am I to say to them? Please give me the words."

She continued to kneel for several more seconds as she attempted to comprehend this newfound affection that had suddenly graced her soul. A sudden recall lay just beyond her mind's grasp. There was something she had seen or read over the past several hours. "*What was it?*" she thought. She began to replay the events of the night's study as she tried to recollect certain words she had read. She picked up Mr. Strobel's book that Ron had given her and that she had spent the past several hours exploring. She then remembered and opened the front cover of the book. There Ron had written, "To my fellow scientist and friend." He then added a verse from Romans 11:33: "Oh, the depth of the riches, both of the wisdom and knowledge of God! How unsearchable are His judgments and unfathomable His ways!"

She sat in momentary contemplation. A broad smile then came on her face. "Yes. Yes. That's it! I need to hang onto that truth," she exclaimed as she took a pen and feverishly began to scribble words into her notebook. Excitement mingled with confident assurance as she closed her notebook and slipped it into her portfolio. She regained her composure and glanced down at her watch. The time for her presentation was drawing near. She wiped the tears from her face, brushed herself off, checked her hair, and then strolled to the hotel balcony overlooking Lake Geneva. Mont Blanc stood majestically in the distance, appearing as a massive, hallowed sentinel peering over the horizon, affording protection for the citizens below. She briefly spoke with Nora over her phone and then made her way across the street to the convention center.

Dr. Engel stood before the gathered crowd. "And now, help me give a warm hand of welcome to Dr. Suzanne Myers." Enthusiastic applause greeted Suzanne as she walked to the center of the stage.

After thanking the crowd for their attendance, she took a deep breath, broadened her smile, and began her delivery.

CHAPTER 28

JUNE 28, 2030
TWO WEEKS HAVE PASSED SINCE THE GENEVA CONFERENCE
RON AND MONA ARE WITH DR. SUZANNE MYERS AND THE TEAM, ROOM B11 AT KING'S UNIVERSITY

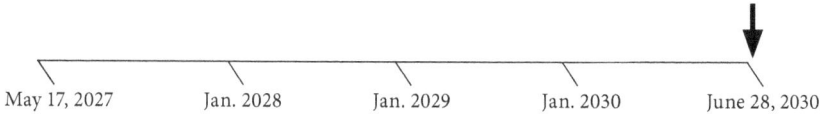

				↓
May 17, 2027	Jan. 2028	Jan. 2029	Jan. 2030	June 28, 2030

Two weeks had passed since the Geneva Science Conference. The team overcame many of the obstacles that kept them from transmitting more complex thoughts from the transmitter to the receiver, even before the date of the Geneva Conference. Simon had developed another electrode skull cap to be worn by the receiver. They were confident in their ability to proceed to the next step in their study and would do so by the following week. On this particular occasion, the team had another purpose in mind. Suzanne wanted to discover for herself whether the neutrino factor held any merit. She and the team were gathered once more in Room B11 of the neuroscience wing of King's University in an attempt to connect the spiritual side of the human condition with that of the neurological nature of the brain. She would soon undergo the same experiment

181

as Erin Roberts and Ron Provost, although each had experienced contradictory effects. Suzanne Myers could find no natural cause for such contradictory outcomes.

Although Ron had not yet voiced a complete analysis of his own experience, it was apparent to every member of the team that what he underwent was akin to nothing short of paradise. Ron believed that his faith in Christ was the major contributing cause to what he had experienced. Suzanne was becoming more convinced of Ron's conviction that neutrinos had actually skimmed God's eternal realm and were thus attracted to the Spirit that indwells believers in Christ. She realized his analysis might hold merit. She could find no other explanation. Such a line of reasoning ran contrary to her neurological training and perspective. Still, she could find no naturalistic cause to explain such phenomena. Her newfound faith in Christ changed her whole perspective on the condition of mankind as well as her own relationship with this One who exists outside His universe and yet is as close as a prayer. She believed her analysis was correct but knew that even if this day's experiment went the way she hoped, it would be inconclusive. She would be hard-pressed to convince the scientific community of her findings. Regardless, she resolved to know the answer. So here she sat waiting to embark on a mystical journey of discovery. Suzanne sat in the comfortable recliner. Nora, Ron, and Mona were keeping her company while Simon, Andreas, and Randall were in the adjacent room making final preparations.

An eerie silence hung in the air, devoid of the usual clamor of traffic and people scurrying about. Here in their basement quarters, the absence of sunshine, replaced by artificial light only, brought on a sense of melancholy. Suzanne was anxious, wondering what was in store. Her thoughts took her back to the Geneva Conference and an unanswered question. "Ron, you never told us why you chose not to share your experience while at the Geneva Conference. You shared a little with our team, so why a change of heart?"

Ron knew that Dr. Myers would eventually ask this question and had considered his answer. This seemed to be the appropriate time as

Suzanne was about to embark on the same journey, hopefully, the same as his. He scooted his chair away from the table. He often made use of arm motions as he spoke. "Dr. Myers, I . . ."

Suzanne interrupted him. "Ron, I think by now we should disregard the formalities, even here. Just call me Suzanne." Mona and Nora gave a knowing smile.

"Okay. Suzanne, allow me to first explain a little more about my experience with the neutrino study. I related to you some of the things I saw but not entirely what I felt, which was the more substantial experience. What happened to me was unlike anything I have ever experienced. Just imagine that you were wrapped up tight with ropes or straps for years if you will. Then suddenly those bonds were released and you experienced total freedom. I felt a sensation of release."

"Release? Really? Is that all?"

"No. There was much more. Now try to imagine a total sense of well-being. No pain. No stress. Total peace. Then on top of that, I experienced a sensation of total love—unconditional love and forgiveness." He looked at Suzanne who furrowed her brows as she appeared confused. "In other words, I think we all carry around with us a sense of uneasiness about all the mistakes we have made in our past. Maybe we hold onto guilt and shame. I think that subconsciously we are waiting for someone to bring accusations against us. I don't know. Anyway, what I experienced was total freedom from all of that. My physical condition, my mental and emotional condition, and my spiritual condition were all made whole. And that sense of unconditional love and forgiveness was overwhelming." Ron paused for a moment.

Suzanne looked at him, still waiting for an explanation for why he would not share this extraordinary experience with the world. "So again, why did you hold back telling all this at the conference? I mean, the whole world would want to hear this."

"Right. Well, you see, knowing that everyone is desperately searching for an escape from the stress and cares of this life is partly why I held back voicing my experience. We want a life of no pain, no guilt, and no shame. Let's face it. We all want to feel a sense of well being. That's why there is alcoholism, psychotropic drugs and other mind-altering drugs, and risky adventures. You know?"

"Yes. I think I know where you are going with this."

"And consider why we all do the things we do. We are searching for an elusive utopia. We go through divorces and failed relationships. We strive for more pleasures in life, so we buy more expensive houses and cars, and strive for success to feel significant. We're looking for that miracle cure for everything that ails us. Our health deteriorates, and we want to feel good, but age finally catches up with us. We are never satisfied. We look to every kind of idol—God replacements, so to speak—to bring us a sense of peace and happiness." Ron saw that Suzanne was beginning to grasp his meaning. "So if I were to come along and tell people about what I found through my encounter with those tiny particles, which I propose reflect the eternal realm, well, let's face it, it would become an idol. Everyone would bombard the university or even us, wanting to know more about this miracle cure."

Suzanne thought for a moment. "You know, Ron, I never thought about that. But you are so right. This might just become the next drug. And even if they experience this euphoria, afterward their life would seem meaningless. Depression might set in, and who knows where that would lead? So, Ron, what about you? Did you experience a letdown afterward?"

"Immediately after that experience, I wanted to go back and do it all over again. But Suzanne, the very fact that I have a relationship with Jesus my Savior helped me know my ultimate hope is in Him, not in what just happened to me. I also know from God's Word that God uses the cares and troubles of this life to build godly character. We learn to trust Him more."

Mona chimed in. "Suzanne, on our ride back home, I remember looking over at Ron, and he had a kind of glow about him. He had this contented smile on his face. He continued to beam for the remainder of the day, but in time, it left him. Ron, can I tell her about . . ."

"Of course. Go ahead. I don't mind at all."

Mona continued. "Ron began to sob uncontrollably. I have never seen him do that before. I asked him what was wrong, and he just said the tears were a mixture of . . . what was it, Ron?"

"Joy and sadness."

Nora now spoke up. "How can you have both joy and sadness at the same time?"

Ron looked intently at Nora. "In addition to my experience, my mind took me back to an event that happened to me when I was eight years old."

Everyone stared expectantly at Ron. By this time, Simon had walked into the room. Ron felt a little uneasy as if he were on display. This life experience he would share was quite personal, and he did not know how it would come across to those present in the room. He directed his eyes toward Mona, who gave him a reassuring nod.

Ron gave them a warning. "This is kind of a long story. Are you sure you all want to hear it? Simon, how about you? How are we doing on time?"

"We're okay, buddy. Let's hear it."

"Well, all right." Ron stood for a moment and stretched his arms over his head as he glanced upward. He then sat back down and began his story. "When I was eight years old, I asked my father if I could go with my friend to a certain movie. Several other friends were also going, and I was really excited about joining them. But my dad said no. He said the movie was inappropriate. I was furious and let him and my mother know in no uncertain terms. I made quite a display of my anger. So they sent me to my room. That just made me even angrier. I stewed in my anger and then decided to get back at my father. By now my father had left to go to meet a customer or something like that."

Nora spoke up. "What does this have to do with sadness and joy?"

"I'm coming to that. It has to do with the unconditional love and forgiveness I spoke of earlier." Nora and the others motioned for him to continue.

"My father had a study where he kept a few items on a shelf. One of them was an old pewter flower vase containing some withered flowers. This vase was my father's prized possession. Every year on a certain day he would change the flowers for some new ones of the same kind, which would eventually fade and die. I hated that vase and thought it was ugly and ridiculous that my father would keep such an ugly old thing containing withered flowers. So I took the vase off the shelf, went outside, threw away the flowers, and began to hammer on it, putting several dents in it. I then flung it into the backyard.”

Simon commented. “I’m thinking your dad gave you quite a whippin’ when he got home, huh?”

“You would think so, but no. He did something remarkable. Mom saw what I had done and sat me down on the sofa. She scolded me with some stern words. By that time, I was feeling quite a lot of shame and guilt and was expecting my father to come down hard on me. My mom said that when Dad got home, she would tell him what happened, but then she told me to expect to hear a story behind the significance of that vase.” Ron hesitated to continue until he could see that he still held everyone’s interest. Suzanne could sense Ron’s reluctance to go on. “Ron, I can assure you, we’re all waiting to hear the end of the story.”

“All right, so my father came home. I saw Mom approach him. As she spoke with him, I could see tears forming in his eyes. The sight of that shook me. He then slowly approached me and sat down next to me on the sofa. He looked over at me with kindness on his face as he related to me a story from long ago. Back in the spring of 1944, my grandfather and his father ran a bakery in a town in southern France known as Auvers. This mountainous region was home to French Resistance fighters known as the Maquis du Mont Mouchet. My grandfather was 18 at the time. His name was Tumas Provost. My great-grandfather would gather armaments that were dropped from British aircraft into selected areas outside Auvers. He would then bring them to a shed behind the bakery where they had a secret compartment where they stored the arms for later distribution.”

“What was your great-grandfather’s name?” Nora asked.

“Varden,” answered Ron. “His name was Varden. Anyway, Varden was reluctant to bring along Tumas when he ventured out to pick up smuggled armaments. Tumas wanted to fight for the Resistance, but my great-grandmother would not have it. Varden insisted Tumas remain at the shop in order not to bring suspicion to the family. By that time, the Milice fighters—German sympathizers—were rounding up the Maquis Resistance fighters and killing many. It was an extremely dangerous time. Several surrounding villages had even been massacred. There was a florist whose shop was adjacent to my great-grandfather's bakery. The owner also had a son about the same age as my grandfather. Their last name was Auguste. Both the man and his son were named Jean. Jean's family did not want to be involved in the Resistance. Even though they sympathized with the cause, they felt the Resistance would only bring tragedy to the community. They were also strong in their faith in the Lord. They knew about my father's involvement in smuggling arms to fighters. Mr. Auguste tried to talk my father out of involvement in the Resistance, but Varden so despised the Germans that he disregarded any warning. Mr. Auguste could see that Varden and Tumas were intent on supplying arms, so he turned a blind eye to what was going on."

"So, what happened?" Simon was anxious to hear more.

"Varden had smuggled supplies on two occasions. Even though he knew it was dangerous, he felt that all had gone well. So, on the third occasion, he allowed Tumas to accompany him on an outing. He asked the Auguste family to watch over the shop. They often did that for one another. While Varden and Tumas were out one evening, the Milice somehow got word of the smuggling operation. They swarmed the bakery, found the secret stash of arms, and arrested both Mr. Auguste and his son." Ron had to take a break to catch his breath. Tears were forming. "Please forgive me."

Suzanne spoke softly. "That's okay, Ron. We realize this is hard for you. When you are ready, go on with the rest of the story. We're all still eager to hear what happened." Everyone in the room nodded in agreement.

Ron took a deep breath and then exhaled slowly as he gathered his resolve to continue. "So, my grandfather and great-grandfather arrived back at the shop. By that time, the Milice had left. Varden and Tumas received word about what had happened and were devastated. My great-grandfather wanted to turn himself in. But my great-grandmother said it would only bring death to our family and probably would not save the Auguste men anyway. Everyone in the village knew just how brutal this Milice faction was. They were known for killing entire villages in order to scare other communities into submission."

"What happened to Mr. Auguste and his son?" Nora suspected the answer.

"They killed Jean Jr. and sent Jean Sr. to a concentration camp."

"Go ahead and tell them about the vase and flowers." Mona knew this was the main point of the story.

Ron gathered his emotions and thoughts. "Okay. So, after the Allies liberated France in the fall of 1944, Jean Auguste Sr. survived imprisonment and came back home. By that time, my great-grandfather had closed his shop, probably out of shame. He went to work somewhere else, as did Tumas. But Mr. Auguste's wife and other children continued the floral shop. Jean Auguste came to the Provost's home one evening. My grandfather, Tumas, answered the door and was petrified to see Mr. Auguste standing there. 'Is your father home?' Jean asked. He held something behind his back. Tumas wondered if it might be a gun but also knew it was unlikely that this man of faith would take vengeful action against his father. Still, Tumas could not imagine any motive other than revenge that would bring this man to their door. 'Father!' he called out. 'Yes, who is it?' Tumas gave him no answer. Instead, Mr. Auguste called out, 'Varden, it's me.'

"My great-grandfather stood speechless before this man, this innocent man who had lost his son, his only son who had done nothing wrong. On top of that, Mr. Auguste had lost half a year of his own life to the German Reich. Finally, Jean Auguste spoke up. 'You must know,' he said, 'that I do not hold any ill will toward you.' He pulled a pewter vase containing a batch of red irises from behind his back and handed it to my great-grandfather. Varden fell to his knees and cried out, 'Oh, Jean, I am so very sorry. I was so wrong. How can you ever forgive me?' Tumas, my grandfather, watched this entire scene take place. He placed his hand on his father's shoulder and through his tears looked up at Mr. Auguste who stepped toward Tumas and then knelt alongside Varden, placing his arm around my great-grandfather as he said, 'I forgive you, my dear friend. This terrible war has caused too much division already.' Tumas also knelt down and then took the vase of flowers from his father's hands. By that time my great-grandmother had entered the room. She, too, dropped to her knees and began to sob. Jean Auguste then uttered a short prayer. He spoke of God's forgiveness and grace. He spoke of God's own Son who had given His own life to bring us back to the Father. There was much sadness mixed with joy that evening." Ron then turned toward Nora who was wiping tears from her eyes. "Do you understand now, Nora, what I meant by sorrow mixed with joy?"

"Yes, I get it now," she answered and then remarked, "So that was the vase you tried to destroy?"

"Yes. My grandfather eventually had it engraved with these words: 'He took my place.' Ever since then, on the anniversary of that day, my family has always placed new flowers in the vase. It is a story and a tradition that my own children now participate in."

Simon spoke up. "So, what did your dad do?" He was still curious about what happened to Ron.

"Well, Simon, my father had me join him in the workshop as he attempted to hammer the pewter vase back in shape. That was punishment enough just to watch him try to correct the terrible wrong I had committed. Then after hearing about the history behind it . . . well, it actually changed my life. Eventually, I began to understand what 'He took my place' meant. Not only had Jean Jr. taken the place of my grandfather but I began to understand the significance of what God, through Christ His own Son, did for me."

Ron held his hands out as if receiving God's gift of forgiveness. He then closed his hands, lowered his arms, and continued. "While I may have had a mental acceptance of my salvation from sin, the incident with the vase helped me fully grasp that love and forgiveness from my eternal Father. It was that sensation of love and forgiveness I experienced that day from the effects of the neutrinos."

Suzanne turned to face both Ron and Mona. "Hey, you two. I have something to confess. I want you to know that I, too, have experienced that same love and forgiveness from Christ. You both helped me to finally see what God's Spirit was revealing to my heart. I made the decision to receive and trust Christ moments before I spoke at the Geneva Conference." Ron and Mona immediately embraced Suzanne.

Mona cheerfully declared, "Welcome to the family, dear sister."

Dr. Randall Milton walked into the room and announced, "It's time, Suzanne."

Suzanne looked up at Dr. Milton through tear-filled eyes. She then glanced slowly around the room, pausing as she studied the faces of those in the room.

"There's no need," she uttered softly. Dr. Milton looked puzzled. Everyone else in the room appeared to understand her decision as they gave her a reassuring smile. Suzanne slowly rose from the comfort of the recliner where she had anxiously awaited the interaction with those mysterious neutrinos. Everyone remained silent, expecting further instructions from their respected colleague. All realized she had persisted through this pioneering study into the deepest recesses of the human mind and thought. Where would she now lead them? Dr. Suzanne Myers brought her hands to her mouth in a prayerful position. She thought for a moment and then spoke. "I've come to realize that the answers I've been looking for do not lie within the bounds of creation or even through the tiniest known particle in creation skimming the very edge of eternity." She looked at Ron and Mona Provost who were nodding in agreement. "As a scientist, I will join my colleagues in exploring further the wonders of God's creation." She then added, "And I will do this knowing the very One who created it all." Suzanne was trying to recall the words the Apostle Paul wrote to the Colossian church. "I read from my Bible early this morning. Let me see if I get it right, 'through Christ lie all the . . . um . . .'"

Ron spoke up. "Hold on, Suzanne." He pulled out his phone and opened an app. "It's a powerful passage." He handed Suzanne his phone that was open to the second chapter of Colossians. "Here, I like the way the NIV version puts it."

Suzanne perused the first few verses. She was about to read verses two and three but was taken by the relevance of verse four. "Oh my!" She looked around the room. The entire team had walked into the room when they heard Suzanne mention the decision not to follow through with the day's test. All eyes were focused on her. "I was going to begin in verse two, but look at what verse four says. This is the Apostle Paul speaking to the Colossian church. 'I tell you this so that no one may deceive you by fine-sounding arguments.'" She looked around to see if the words spoken seemed to affect others as they did for her. She could not be certain. She continued. "Now here's what it says in verse two. Paul wanted everyone to have, quote, 'the full riches of complete understanding, in order that they may know the mystery of God, namely, Christ, in whom are hidden all the treasures of wisdom and knowledge.'"

She handed the phone back to Ron and thought to herself, *"I wonder. Did they truly get that?"*

A New Beginning

PARADIGMS

Proposing an alternative perspective for evaluating the existence of God and His revelation to the world

Richlon Merrill

Paradigms

David Blaine is an illusionist. Like most illusionists, his job is to convince you that what you might claim is impossible just occurred before your very eyes. David Blaine is most commonly known as a street magician and often performs his "magic" using a deck of cards where his up close and personal style creates an even greater sense of astonishment among the small crowd of spectators. If you have ever witnessed his feats, you, too, would begin to question your previously held beliefs about reality. But David would readily admit that he uses your commonly held beliefs against you to convince you that the impossible just occurred. If he were to explain how he accomplished his illusion, you would suddenly come to realize that your initial perspective was wrong. He would have provided you with another paradigm, a different perspective. Your eyes would have been opened to a new truth because you used a different method to examine that truth.

All of us like to think that we perceive our world correctly. We don't like being told we are wrong. If we are ever going to know the truth about anything, we must first humble ourselves and admit that we may not hold all the right answers.

The purpose of this book is to help you gain a new perspective on how you evaluate the existence and revelation of God, the One who is the ultimate possessor of and authority on truth.

I want to challenge you with the following claims.

God does not need or even desire to prove His existence to you.

You might be thinking, who am I to speak for God? Nevertheless, I assert that those trusting in their innate ability to scrutinize the existence of God may need to embrace that statement before it is even possible to come to the truth concerning God's existence, much less the truth He wants us to embrace. For although God has provided ample evidence for His existence and his message to humanity, there is a greater quandary at hand.

Just as a magician must redirect your perspective to a different paradigm to reveal his or her secrets, in the same way, the entire subject concerning God's existence must be approached from an entirely different paradigm, or perspective, than the one many people use in drawing their conclusions. In a sense, this is the challenge I am making.

The false assumption is that people must somehow obtain enough evidence to convince them that God exists.

That is the old paradigm and must shift *before a realization of the truth is even possible*. The problem is not for lack of evidence. The search for evidence will bring clear verification. *Evidence for God is overwhelming*. It includes cosmological, microbiological, historical, and archaeological evidence that supports the claims of Scripture. Scientific discovery, too, will reveal evidence for our Creator God. Additionally, scriptural preservation through a chain of custody and textual criticism of the biblical text reveals the consistent preservation of the biblical text. Internal biblical evidence such as fulfilled prophecies, the consistent unity of the message throughout the Bible, and external sources of Scripture verify its authenticity. The evidence is abundant and could be brought forward, but that is not the main intent of this book. There is a bounty of publications that address this evidence for those who seek it. If evidence is what you seek, then start seeking. But the evidence is not the issue. The snag comes in our reliance on a potentially flawed, four-pound mass of tissue between our ears—our brain—as our *final* authority in judging the truth of God's existence. How much evidence is enough to satisfy you? How much evidence is enough to satisfy others? Maybe you have weighed enough evidence to conclude that God does not exist and wonder how any intelligent person could conclude otherwise. Believers in God are delusional, you say. If God were real, then surely, He would make Himself apparent to all. I would suggest to you that all our greatest tools of discovery and even God's best undeniable and verifiable evidence are still not enough to overcome the real issue that has nothing to do with the determination of God's existence. Once the subject is approached from a different paradigm, you may come to realize that God planned it that way all along. Perhaps at this point, you are expecting me to say something along the lines of "therefore we must simply have faith that He exists." No, that is not my assertion, which is because *the matter regarding God's existence is not resolved by our inborn ability to resolve it.* Keep tracking with me.

The difficulty in discovering God stems from our inward nature.
In other words (and this is an easy point to believe), people everywhere are messed up. Our inborn nature, along with the influence of the culture around us, has tainted our minds, our choices, our affections, and our emotions. On top of that, everyone is left with his or her interpretation of the truth. Much of the world's problems are, in part, due to this fact. I assert that all of mankind does not have the ability to make a grand, unified, truthful, and good conclusion about anything—*anything*! Everyone's mind is like a computer that has been corrupted by a virus. It cannot correctly process data.

The prophet Jeremiah wrote, "The heart is more deceitful than all else and is desperately sick; who can understand it?" (Jer. 17:9). Do you doubt that? Not only does the Bible make this claim, but an honest appraisal of society substantiates this truth. Consider the deception under Nazi-controlled Germany, racism and segregation in America, or mass suicides in cult religions. For centuries, the Roman Catholic Church kept a deceptive hold on the hearts and minds of millions. Now consider that you, too, may have been deceived in various ways. In Paul's letter to the Romans, he says, "Rather, God must prove to be true, though every person *be found* a liar" (Rom. 3:4).

God alone is righteous and true—not us. In a society that promotes relative truth, one person's right is another person's wrong. One person's truth is another person's error. I would suggest that this wretched state we are in is an obvious fact, but even that would be challenged by someone. I am hoping that you and I can agree on that.

Who is on the throne?

Picture this. One day you are going about your daily routine when suddenly a massive, glowing being standing thousands of feet high, well up into the clouds, appears before you. Maybe He appears before everyone. His majesty is so great that it knocks you to your knees. You are blinded by the glorious light. You fear for your life, but then He suddenly smiles at you, and it's even kind of reassuring. You might be thinking to yourself, "Hey, self, could this be God?" And then He opens His mouth to speak. His voice is so loud that you have to hold your hands over your ears. It's like thunder. He says, "I am God!" By this point, you are thinking that maybe He is who He says He is. But you're still not convinced, so you think, "Maybe He should perform a few miracles." That might just do the trick to convince you that He is God. So you dream up your best set of miracles. One is that He must know what you are thinking and tell you so. And sure enough, He knows what you are thinking. He performs the miracles you were thinking about, which should nail down the coffin in the unbelief department. He even goes well beyond your expectations. He creates another moon right in front of you. He then explains all of history to you, to the extent that you are saying to yourself, "Oh, now I get it. He has explained everything and answered all my hard questions, and now I finally have all the criteria I need to believe that He exists." So you tell Him so. You let Him know that He has finally convinced you of His existence. You even shout it from the mountaintop. *"I believe that God exists!"* Hallelujah and all that stuff. But then He does something unexpected. He suddenly looks at you sternly and announces in His thunderous voice, "I banish you to hell." And so, now you're in hell. What?

Who is submitting to whom?

Wow! Some loving good God He turned out to be. But in case you haven't figured it out yet, in this particular scenario, we must ask who was on the throne of judgment. *Who was submitting to whom?* I would suggest to you that you were trying to take the place of God. *You were acting as a judge over God*, expecting Him to meet your particular criteria for belief. So, the fact is that you were not submitting to God at all but were expecting Him to have to submit to you. You had your criteria for belief. He met it, and you then decided He was worthy of your belief. It might be compared to a two-year-old requiring the parent to submit to his or her authority and way of thinking. The parent doesn't have to prove anything to the two-year-old. And yet that is what many unbelievers do. They want God to conform to their imagined criteria. Keep in mind that they are relying on a four-pound mass of tissue between their ears in making this judgment. If intelligence were the deciding factor, then those with the largest amount of grey matter would be found more worthy of God's acceptance. Since God is the One who gave you that brain, then He still gets to make the call. He knows you better than you know yourself. He knows what's going on inside that brain. He knows just how messed up you are. Do you?

So again, I ask you: Who was submitting to whom? Oh, and by the way, all those thousands or perhaps millions or billions of others who saw this giant God may have been saying to themselves, "He'd better meet my particular criteria for belief or I'm not going to believe." They, too, were relying on that four-pound mass of tissue between their ears as their final authority for determining the truth. Even still, the Bible states that God has given us all the evidence and revelation we need so that all of creation is silenced and everyone is without excuse. God does, in fact, expect us to respond and receive His revelation. Here's one such passage from the book of Romans.

> For the wrath of God is revealed from heaven against all ungodliness and unrighteousness of men who suppress the truth in unrighteousness, because that which is known about God is evident within them; for God made it evident to them. For since the creation of the world His invisible attributes, His eternal power, and divine nature, have been clearly seen, being understood through what has been made, so that they are without excuse.
>
> Rom. 1:18–20 NASB 1995

This inborn nature that prevents everyone from acknowledging and submitting to this evidence from God has a name.
It's called the sin nature. The word *sin* in Scripture is defined as "missing the mark" and refers to any transgression of God's laws. Sin goes way beyond missing a target. The fact is that we aren't even trying to hit a target. Each of us has been born with a soul that is engrossed in rejection of God's righteousness. We live with ourselves on the throne of our life. We are the captains of our own souls.

The Bible describes God as both just and loving. Many unbelievers would scoff at this characterization. They do so because they look at the world around them with all the pain, suffering, and tragedy and can only conclude that it must mean that there is no such thing as a perfect, loving God. How could a loving, perfect God allow all the injustice, death, and pain in the world? This, too, needs to be addressed. We'll come back to that, but let's stay on point for now.

God said, "It is good."

The first book of the Bible, Genesis, begins by describing God's act of creation. After He makes the Earth, He says it is "good." After He makes the heavens, He says it is "good." Each time He creates something else, He always follows it by saying it is "good." The account ends by declaring, "God saw all that He had made, and behold, it was very good" (Gen. 1:31). So far, all God created might be compared to a pure glass of water. There were no impurities in it whatsoever. It was a pure glass of water, and it was "good." God eventually created a man and a woman and clearly stated His requirements governing His creation. He knows that as long as they are followed, everything He created will continue to remain good, whole, and in perfect harmony. That perfect world we all yearn for today, and then blame God for when we see that it isn't, was pure, loving, whole, and . . . "good."

But then there is that unfortunate episode in the Garden of Eden. Don't write off this subject without examining closely the implications. The fact is that God gave our distant relatives, Adam and Eve, a choice not just to obey Him from a sense of duty but to make a heart choice to love and trust Him. Then that fateful hour occurred when they disobeyed. Couldn't God have just let it go? Surely it was no big thing. Think back to the water illustration. I don't care how big and pure that glass of water is. If you were to drop even the tiniest drop of sulfuric acid into it, then it would no longer be perfect, whole, and "good." That impurity will always be there. Well, okay, I'm sure the water department folks know how to do it, but you get the point. The fact is that the willful choice made by Adam and Eve changed everything and is still playing itself out today. By the way, look at Eve's reasoning. "When the woman saw that the fruit of the tree was good for food and pleasing to the eye, and also desirable for gaining wisdom, she took some and ate it" (Gen. 3:6 NIV). The same thing is still going on today, except we might call it the lust of the eyes (that thing sure looks good to me), the lust of the flesh (that thing sure makes me feel good.), and the pride of life (that position of power and success sure would make me feel significant).

At the heart of each of these desires is the dissatisfaction with the good God provides. Lust and control take over and push God's provision aside. The Bible goes on to explain that since God is pure, righteous, just, loving, and holy, He simply cannot allow anything impure or unrighteous to be tolerated. It would be as if a cancer has invaded the body and must be eliminated or death will occur. The condition of the world and society throughout history attest to the fact that things are corrupt. God's perfect holiness cannot allow it to remain so forever in His presence. His laws and His very being are so absolutely holy and perfect that we simply cannot stand in His presence. We would be consumed by that holiness and be destroyed just as fire consumes all impurities. He is righteous and just and can do no wrong. He is the perfect Creator and Judge. If He says we are guilty and sinful, then we are. We try to rationalize and come up with some other explanation. We may want to try to give God some sort of human characteristics to conform to our way of thinking. *We reach up and try to bring God down to our level.*

Humans are finite. God is infinite.

Let's imagine that we all live on a two-dimensional plane. Three dimensions do not exist in our world. We are like line drawings on a piece of paper. That is all our brains and our world will allow us to conceive. But what if a fingertip were to come down on that two-dimensional field? Keep in mind that we cannot see that it is anything other than a big, flat blob in our two-dimensional world. That illustrates what we try to do with God. We try to use the limited resources He has given us in our physical world to try to explain something our minds cannot conceive. And it drives us crazy. Where did time begin? How can it possibly end? Where does the universe begin? How can it possibly end? Yeah, go ahead and chew on those questions for a while. So when it comes to the eternal God, why do we continue to think we can figure Him out? If He doesn't stand up to our criteria for rational thinking, then we figure this four-pound mass of tissue between our ears (which He put there, by the way, and gave it the limitations as He determined best) must be a higher authority than Him.

Dwell on that end of time and universe thing a little while longer, and then continue to tell me you can figure things out . . . much less God. Do you think science is the end all? God is the One who established the scientific laws of nature. God is eternal and beyond time and matter. After all, He created time and matter. He is the dimension we cannot fathom. God laughs at our futile attempts to deny His power and authority. "He who sits in the heavens laughs, the Lord scoffs at them" (Ps. 2:4). Oh, the arrogance of people! God, not mankind, is the One who holds all truth. Our ideas of relative truth just won't stand up alongside God's authority and ultimate truth.

God is both just and merciful, but how can He be both at the same time?

Since there is no higher authority than God, He gets to decide what is right and wrong and determines the penalty for sin. And that whole penalty for sin thing simply comes, once again, with the fact that nothing unholy and impure can remain in His presence. It's just a tragic fact—that drop of acid in the glass of water thing or the cancer in the body thing. Look at what this "cancer" (sin) has done to our society and world. Now try to imagine if it were to remain so for all eternity. But this cancer, this sin-filled world, has been a reality from day one (in a manner of speaking). Why is God continuing to allow all this injustice to remain in the world? When should final judgment begin? Where should He begin to right all wrongs? Should He begin with me . . . or how about you? Will you stand up against God's rightful verdict against sin? The verdict is in. "For all have sinned and fall short of the glory of God" (Rom. 3:23).

How am I ever to be found good enough to stand before this holy God? How am I to justify my defiance of His authority? Do I stand on the grounds of my own goodness? If goodness and self-effort were the determining factors for acceptance by God, then pride would immediately rear its ugly head and proclaim, "Look at me and how worthy I am to stand before this holy, righteous God." The arrogance of this position immediately negates its claim.

God has plans for eternity, and they do not include prideful, self-centered humans who are only concerned with their self-interests and unable to see God because of their inward, tainted sin nature.

Governing this bleak picture is a God who is supposed to encompass love. Well, let's see. He is just, so it only reasons that a perfect judge will judge sin perfectly. You can argue all day long that "God made me this way," but that isn't going to change the fact that you fall tremendously short of a righteous God and His decrees. Can you admit that? But if He also encompasses perfect love, then what is the remedy for this dichotomy?

The answer is Jesus Christ.
If Jesus is the solution to this dilemma, then we must understand who He is and why He came into the world. Many passages make His identity known. Here is one such passage. Please consider carefully your response to its claim.

> *He is the image of the invisible God, the firstborn of all creation: for by Him all things were created, both in the heavens and on earth, visible and invisible, whether thrones, or dominions, or rulers, or authorities—all things have been created through Him and for Him. He is before all things, and in Him all things hold together. He is also the head of the body, the church; and He is the beginning, the firstborn from the dead, so that He Himself will come to have first place in everything. For it was the* Father's *good pleasure for all the fullness to dwell in Him, and through Him to reconcile all things to Himself, whether things on earth or things in heaven, having made peace through the blood of His cross.*
>
> Col. 1:15–20

The first words written by the Apostle John in his account of the life and ministry of Jesus reveal much about this man. He writes, "In the beginning was the Word, and the Word was with God, and the Word was God. He was in the beginning with God. All things came into being through Him, and apart from Him nothing came into being that has come into being" (John 1:1–3 NASB 1995). By using the title "the Word," John is indicating that this Jesus was the entire Word of God summed up and revealed in flesh. "And the Word became flesh, and dwelt among us" (John 1:14 NASB 1995). Quite a claim, wouldn't you agree?

Through these accounts and many more, we are presented with the deity of Jesus. That is why he is called the Christ. Jesus didn't come down from heaven as a cosmic celestial being but was born as a man into time and space by the Spirit of God. God placed His seed, His Spirit, into Mary's womb. She conceived a man, just like you and me, except that He was not born from Adam's seed, which was carried down through the generations to Joseph, Mary's husband. If he had been born from Joseph's seed, he would have that same sinful nature that you and I have. But Jesus still had to live the same life as you and me, making the same kinds of choices, facing the same temptations. This is a crucial point. He had to be both *fully human and fully divine*. Where His humanity is concerned, those desires to satisfy the eyes, the flesh, and the pride of life came against Him, just as they do for you and me. If you read the narrative about Satan's temptations while Jesus was on his 40-day fast in the desert before beginning His earthly ministry, you'll see that the three temptations fall under those same old tried and true temptations that faced Eve as well as you and me—lust of the eyes, lust of the flesh, and pride of life. Yet Jesus never sinned. "He [Jesus Christ] who committed no sin, nor was any deceit found in His mouth" (1 Pet. 2:22).

He remained in constant connection with His Father. He followed all the laws of God and carried them out perfectly. They were wrapped up in Him. Again, recall that the Apostle John called Him "the Word" (John 1:1). Christians gain a great deal of joy seeing this portrayed throughout Scripture in both the Old and New Testaments. In fact, some smarter people than I have said that there are over 300 prophecies, typologies, illustrations, and analogies concerning the coming of Christ, this Messiah, and all of them are fulfilled in this one man. That's right. His mission, His life, and His very being and nature are shown throughout all Old Testament Scriptures leading up to this coming Messiah. Jesus wasn't a man who began a new religion. He wasn't just some prophet or inspirational teacher as some might suggest. He was and is divine in every respect. Scripture makes this truth abundantly clear. The sin nature rejects this truth because it knows it must give an account to that truth. The sin nature wants to define its own set of values and truth. The Bible states that since all mankind is sinful and deserving of hell, then a penalty for this sin must be paid. Perfect justice demands it. Someone did, indeed, pay that debt that you and I owe.

The great exchange

Jesus, the sinless "man," took our place on a cross and paid that penalty of sin. "This is love: not that we loved God, but that he loved us and sent his Son as an atoning sacrifice for our sins" (1 John 4:10 NIV). His death satisfied the debt we owe for our guilt. And make no mistake about it. You and I and everyone born into this world are guilty before a holy, righteous God. You can *never* be good enough through your own efforts to be reconciled to God and have Him reveal his full presence to you. You might at this point throw yourself into a great gulf of sorrow and tell yourself that you are going to live for God. But even that won't gain you access to God because you would still be depending on your own effort.

What will reconcile you to God? Here it is:

> But God demonstrates His own love toward us, in that while we were yet sinners, Christ died for us. Much more then, having now been justified by His blood, we shall be saved from the wrath of God through Him. For if while we were enemies we were reconciled to God through the death of His Son, much more, having been reconciled, we shall be saved by His life.
>
> Rom. 5:8–10

Believe that what Jesus Christ did was the price that had to be paid. Jesus, as a man, represents us. Jesus, as God, represents God. He is our mediator. He purchased you with His blood. Receive that sacrifice, and allow him to *dethrone* you and take His *rightful seat on the throne of your life.*

This plan of God might not make sense to you. Here is an illustration. It's as if you are standing before God, the perfect Judge, and He slams down His gavel and declares you guilty of breaking all His laws and rebelling against His kingship. You are therefore banished from His presence forever in a place designated for demons. He then steps down from behind His bench and comes down to where you are standing. He declares that He will take the place for your punishment and banishment. The One who made the law is also the One who disseminates justice. Not only that, but as the God-Man, He is the *only one* who can do that. No one else is worthy or has the authority.

Since Jesus was born of God being fully divine but also born of a woman being fully human, then that is precisely what took place. Adam, the first man whose defiled nature still resides in all of us, results in our guilt. Jesus, the new Adam, has taken that place in believers, but *only if we will receive Him into our life*, which is not really our life at all, but His.

How, then, am I, this messed up person, ever going to be found worthy to stand before the holy God? It's all about God's grace. God's grace does not mean He turns a kindly old grandfatherly blind eye to what we have done as an offense to Him. No. It means that through God's loving-kindness, He has graciously provided the solution to deal with those offenses. In so doing, *He can reconcile His justice with His love.* We can then be justified before our God who is both perfect love and perfect justice.

Death could not hold Jesus in the grave because Jesus did not sin. He rose, which means the verdict has been dealt with and life was and is now *available to all who place their trust in Christ and His perfect holiness.*

Controlled by the Spirit

The Bible promises that the same Spirit and life that is in Christ will come to live in us when we place our trust in Christ. Check out these passages.

But if the Spirit of Him who raised Jesus from the dead dwells in you, He who raised Christ Jesus from the dead will also give life to your mortal bodies through His Spirit who dwells in you.

Rom. 8:11

Or do you not know that your body is a temple of the Holy Spirit who is in you, whom you have from God, and that you are not your own?

1 Cor. 6:19 NASB 1995

In the 15th chapter of John's Gospel, Jesus is making the analogy that He is the vine that supplies nourishment and growth to the branches, indicating the absolute necessity to remain connected to Him and His life-producing strength. So you see, Jesus, the new Adam, can now occupy our souls. Something marvelous then takes place. You will have a different nature than the one you had previously. Does that mean that you won't continue to mess up and sin? No. It means there is now a Spirit living inside of you that enables you to overcome sin. Your relationship with God will take on a whole new dimension. His love enables you to love Him and desire His presence in your life. The nature you had before simply decided for itself what choices were right or wrong. The sin nature would not and could not submit to God. *It was impossible.*

But a natural man does accept the things of the Spirit of God; for they are foolishness to him, and he cannot understand them, because they are spiritually appraised.

1 Cor. 2:14 NASB 1995

The god of this age [Satan] has blinded the minds of unbelievers, so that they cannot see the light of the gospel that displays the glory of Christ, who is the image of God.

2 Cor. 4:40 NIV

Without God's perfect Spirit living inside of us, we are totally destitute and simply relying on our brain, that four-pound mass of tissue between our ears, to guide us through life—to be our Savior, so to speak. But when we allow Jesus to be our Guide, our Shepherd, and our Savior, we have Him on the inside of us giving us the desire and the ability to live for God.

Maybe this illustration will drive home the point. Perhaps after a night of partying you ended up drinking too much. Once intoxicated, who or what was making your choices? You might say you are still making your choices and must suffer the consequences of those choices. You would be right. Or you might say that it was the alcohol that influenced those choices and therefore shares some blame in the matter. You would be right about that too. Now, similarly, if the Spirit of God is residing within you, then He will affect your desires, your ability to accomplish those desires, and the choices you make. So, what I am saying is that we are living either with the old sin nature governing our choices or with our new, "born again," Spirit-filled nature governing our choices. The choices are still ours to make, and we might not make good ones. But with God's Spirit, we now have the *ability* to make good choices. God's grace continues to work in our lives until He brings us home. If we were suddenly made perfect after receiving Christ, then perhaps pride would once again raise its ugly head, or perhaps we would become a bunch of robots of sorts. God's work in our lives is a process. This process involves suffering and testing. The difference is that these life experiences can be a means of drawing us closer to God rather than creating further division. If we sin, we recognize it and can repent. That can *only* be true for one who has God's Spirit residing within. God's work in us does not end by receiving Christ. It is true that you have been "born again" (John 3:3), or "born from above." That means that you have passed from eternal death to eternal life.

The new nature will give you the desire to know more and more about God, as long as you "do not quench the Spirit" (1 Thess. 5:19), who is performing His work on your heart. We'll have more to say about this later on. It is probably time to point out one important and crucial truth.

If we are to know God, He must reveal Himself to us.

We have already seen that God reveals His eternal power and authority through nature—through His creation. But there are limitations to knowing God solely through His creation. God further extends the revelation of Himself through His Word. He does not give us the option to decide for ourselves who He is. If this were the case, we would be creating a God to our liking. He is God. He gets to decide the *means* and *method* and *medium* by which He reveals Himself.

Our need isn't to try to figure Him out. God declared this through the prophet Isaiah.

> *"For My thoughts are not your thoughts, nor are your ways My ways," declares the* Lord. *"For as the heavens are higher than the earth, so are My ways higher than your ways and My thoughts than your thoughts."*
>
> Isa. 55:8–9

We will never completely understand what He is up to while we are on this Earth. He says, "The secret things belong to the Lord our God" (Deut. 29:29).

He has built into our brains and our world certain limitations. We simply cannot depend on our flawed minds to figure things out and "save" us. Once again, *the problem is sin*. The solution for overcoming this malady and restoring our relationship with God is *through the sacrifice made on our behalf through our sinless Messiah*.

Where does the rubber meet the road? It comes through faith. It comes through *trust that what God has revealed and accomplished we can believe and stand on*—no matter what. No matter what trials and pain life throws at us. No matter who tries to intimidate or harm us, we need to remember that they will hate us because they first hated Jesus (see John 15:18). Those who hated Jesus did so because He claimed the ultimate authority of truth. Christians are often hated for testifying of this One who is the ultimate truth. Despite all the problems we face, we still rely on God and His truth. Even the pain, trials, and mess-ups are part of His means to grow us and make us more like Christ, which is the ultimate goal of the Holy Spirit in our lives.

God has given us His resources.

Once we receive the offer of salvation from Christ, God's Spirit directs us to the resources He has lovingly given us.

One of these is the Bible. You can argue all day long using the limitations of human reasoning that it is merely the compiled writings of mere men, so how can it have come from God? Paul, in a letter written to Timothy, made this claim: "*All Scripture is given by inspiration of God, and is profitable for doctrine, for reproof, for correction, for instruction in righteousness, that the man of God may be complete, thoroughly equipped for every good work (2 Tim. 3:16–17 NKJV).*

In another passage, Paul writes, "For this reason we also constantly thank God that when you received the word of God which you heard from us, you accepted *it* not *as* the word of *mere* men, but as what it really is, the word of God, which also is at work in you who believe" (1 Thess. 2:13).

Jesus, in one of his prayers to the Father, said, "Your word is truth" (John 17:17). *There are over 3,000 instances throughout the whole of Scripture where we read,* "The Lord said" *or* "The Lord spoke" *or other such phrases.* I ask you, are you willing to rely on that brain of yours with all its limitations and faults to refute all 3,000 of these claims? Or do you, like so many others who have erroneously tried and failed to do so, try to dissect Scripture in an attempt to find contradictions and errors? Do you stand on your own intelligence and ability to reason and explain away biblical authority and truth? Stop for a moment, and consider God's plan.

God used a certain man, Abraham, and his descendants as His vehicle to bring the revelation of Himself to all people. He chose the Jewish nation. They did not initially choose Him. God set in motion the history (His story) of this nation of Abraham's descendants with the declaration that through them He would bring about the One who would bring about salvation from sin and reconciliation with God. That nation is, of course, Israel. From the first words found in Genesis through the last words of Malachi, God began to reveal His words and plan for redeeming mankind, using those individuals He chose to use, utilizing the very bents, gifts, talents, and statuses in their individual times, but then through the inspiration of the Holy Spirit (authored by God) to pen the words God knew we needed to hear.

Here is an illustration. Suppose you were walking along a path and noticed a line of ants spread out in the field along your path. Upon further inspection, you noticed that the line formed by those ants spelled out the words "Give glory to God." You reason to yourself that this cannot be possible, for ants are incapable of doing such a thing. You would be partially right. The ants would not have the capability of presenting such a message on their own. But there it is before you, an intelligible sentence. The sentence gives you a clue to its origin. A vastly superior being must have made this possible and wants all who read it to know its origin. This makes the point that while Scripture was written by men, it had its origin with God.

The entire Bible has the same thread. It has the same unity of message even though it was written by 40 different men from vastly different periods, cultures, and statuses over 1,500 years to bring about this unified message of a coming Redeemer to restore our broken relationship with God.

The writer of the book of Hebrews in the New Testament opens his letter with these words:

> God, after He spoke long ago to the fathers in the prophets in many portions and many ways, but in these last days has spoken to us in His Son, whom He appointed heir of all things, through whom also He made the world. And He is the radiance of His glory and the exact representation of His nature and upholds all things by the word of His power. When He had made purification of sins, He sat down at the right hand of the Majesty on high.
>
> Heb. 1:1–3

In the New Testament, those who now had the Spirit of God living within them began to make that message plain. He then used faithful, Spirit-filled men of God to create the canon of Scripture that we now call the Bible. The books of the Bible were not chosen but rather recognized. The early church fathers simply compiled the books already recognized as being inspired. Using human logic and reasoning, that could not possibly happen. But just as Jesus said, "With people this is impossible, but with God all things are possible" (Matt. 19:26).

The mystery is explained. The message was made clear, but you must go to Him on His terms to hear it. Once you do, the understanding, the revelation from God, continue to develop in your heart and mind throughout your lifetime. Your rebellious heart of stone softens and changes. "Moreover, I will give you a new heart and put a new spirit within you; and I will remove the heart of stone from your flesh and give you a heart of flesh" (Ezek. 36:26).

We who place our trust in Jesus Christ have the awesome privilege of reading those words and having the Spirit reveal the truth to us. Once again, the Bible says that the natural man—or those who are perishing, as Scripture puts it—cannot understand the words of God. They are foolishness to them. The natural man decides which parts are worthy to be read and then tries to interpret them to line up with his or her perspective on life and notions of truth. In most cases, the natural man simply ignores God's revelation and creates his or her ideas of religion or truth or morality, which seem good to him or her.

Another resource is His church. The church is not a building or a religious organization. It is *not* a gathering of people who rely on rituals and traditions to somehow make them presume to do good things for God, thinking perhaps that God is impressed by the sound of bells and chants interspersed with chords from a glorious organ. Paul warns believers: "See to it that there is no one who takes you captive through philosophy and empty deception in accordance with human tradition, in accordance with the elementary principles of the world, rather than in accordance with Christ" (Col. 2:8). Later he adds, "These are matters which do have the appearance of wisdom in self-made religion and humility and severe treatment of the body, *but* are of no value against fleshly indulgence" (Col. 2:23). They do not bring about a heart change. This is a man-made religion.

Sadly, many groups who call themselves a church are doing just that. In these churches, the Word of God is rarely scratched below the surface. In contrast, the authentic Christian church is made up of those individuals who *have placed their hope and trust in Christ (the "Word" of God).* They dig deep into the treasure of God's Word and desire to accurately apply it to their lives.

Scripture refers to the church in many different ways. For instance, the church is referred to as the "body of Christ." Christ is the head, and we are His body. Just as our bodies have many different parts that function in unison, we, too, are to be functioning in a variety of ways in the church. *Christian* means "follower of Christ." Christ Himself formed the church, not a Council of Nicaea in AD 325, as some would assert. The church is a resource He lovingly provided. He never intended for us to be a Lone-Ranger type of Christian. It is through the church that God gives feet to His mission and message of salvation. God uses His Word, His church, and His Holy Spirit, accompanied by prayer, to accomplish not only His work in the world but also His work in each believer's life. We must remain connected to Christ, the Word, in order to fulfill God's plan for our lives. We can quench this work when we fail to acknowledge the instruction and teaching from the Word of God. The Holy Spirit works in tandem with the words of Scripture. That is why much of the New Testament *admonishes the Christ follower to study and apply the truths found within the whole of Scripture.* How sad it is that the Roman Catholic Church kept so many in the dark for so long by prohibiting individual reading and studying of Scripture.

We must remain connected to one another—to love, build up, encourage, and admonish one another. We all know those individuals who call themselves Christians but demonstrate no real change in their lives. Unbelievers are quick to point out the hypocrisy of believers. Believers are to exhibit the love and grace of God in all they do. If and when we drift away from Christ and His resources, God's love for us will bring about corrective measures in the life of His children.

It's time to make a choice.

Let me tell you what I believe may happen with you right now. Actually, one of two different things may occur. On the one hand, you may find yourself somewhere between indifferent, annoyed, or even infuriated. Perhaps you are fed up with all this nonsense and continue to believe that Christians have bought into an irrational set of beliefs that defy logic and reasoning. How could we believe all those fairy tales in the Bible? I mean, come on, people. Use the brains that God gave you . . . er, I mean that evolution gave you.

So what if what I am telling you is true? That changes everything. It even changes my motivation for writing this book and suggesting that you need a paradigm shift in the way you approach the existence of God and His purpose for your life.

If not, then once again, you are left as your final authority that brain, that four-pound mass of tissue with neurons making electrochemical transmissions that simply evolved without a Creator over several million years. Good luck with that.

Another thing that might happen is that you give God a chance to enter your heart. He may cause you to humble yourself and admit that you have missed the mark, to see the foolishness of requiring God to prove Himself to you. Perhaps the Spirit of God is bringing you to a point of recognizing your sinful state. You may come to realize that without a Savior, you are destitute and guilty before our holy, righteous God.

In that case, you might simply talk to God and say something along these lines:

> Okay, God. I get it. I admit my arrogance and rejection of You. I am messed up and deserving of whatever consequences You have declared. I have not submitted to You and have ignored Your authority over my life. I've been blind to the obvious evidence of Your power and wisdom and love. I have to admit that my life is a wreck. I am miserable much of the time. And I keep making others' lives miserable as well. If you have said that You can replace my anxiety with peace,

then I will just believe it, even if it doesn't make any sense to me right now. Having realized this and the fact that my sin was what caused Your own Son to have to pay an agonizing price for my sinful condition, I give myself to You. I know You see right through me. I cannot hide anything from You. I stand naked before You. As I said, God, I am guilty. No excuses, God. You've got me.

Almighty God, I am at your mercy.

Now I am choosing to place my trust in what Jesus Christ did for me. I am thankful that His act of obedience now makes it possible for me to stand in Your presence totally forgiven. Oh, my Lord, how I need to hear those words—I am forgiven. Thank You. I am Yours. Show me the next step, Lord. I still have troubling questions that don't make much sense to me right now. I know I need a group of believers surrounding me, loving me, and helping me on my journey. I know they, too, are on a journey and might mess up at times, but give me Your spirit of love and forgiveness. Show me that place, Lord.

God willing and by His grace and mercy, that will happen to you.

If God begins to burden your heart, believe that it is coming from Him. *It means that He desires to reveal Himself to you and bring you into His family.* Even if those nagging questions keep popping up that don't appear to have an answer, don't ignore what God has providentially revealed to you at this time. There's more to come. Surround yourself with others who have experienced this revelation.

If, however, you are not burdened as I described, then perhaps you can at least stop the condescending remarks toward those people who only want to wish you well and who, perhaps, have been praying for you. Besides, they really can't help who they are. *God changed their very nature and gave them the ability and privilege to not only know of Him but to intimately know Him.*

BIBLIOGRAPHY

Ashton, John F. *Evolution Impossible: 12 Reasons Why Evolution Cannot Explain Life on Earth.* Green Forest, AR: Master Books, 2018.

Bergman, Jerry. *Evolution's Blunders, Frauds and Forgeries.* Powder Springs, GA: Creation Book Publishers, 2017.

Creation.com. Accessed July 5, 2022, https://creation.com/.

"DNA Replication – 3D." Yourgenome. June 26, 2015. https://www.youtube.com/watch?v=TNKWgcFPHqw.

"Evidence Supporting Biological Evolution." National Library of Medicine. Accessed March 2022, https://www.ncbi.nlm.nih.gov/books/NBK230201.

"From DNA to Protein – 3D." Yourgenome. January 7, 2015. https://www.youtube.com/watch?v=gG7uCskUOrA.

Geisler, Norman L., and Patrick Zukeran. *The Apologetics of Jesus.* Grand Rapids, MI: Baker Books, 2009.

Guillermo Gonzalez. "The Privileged Planet." Illustra Media. April 19, 2013. https://www.youtube.com/watch?v=8ohuG3Vj_48.

"Gunter Bechly Explains What the Fossil Evidence Really Says." Discovery Science. November 23, 2021. https://www.youtube.com/watch?v=V15sjy7gtVM.

Institute for Creation Research. Accessed July 5, 2022, https://www.icr.org/.

Meyer, Stephen. "Darwin's Doubt." Discovery Science. March 18, 2019. https://www.youtube.com/watch?v=L0-hgSjnomA.

Meyer, Stephen. "DNA and Information – Science Uprising Expert Interview." Discovery Science. June 19, 2019. https://www.youtube.com/watch?v=7c9PaZzsqEg,

Meyer, Stephen. "Dr. Stephen C. Meyer, Ph.D. Talks about the Case for Intelligent Design." Trinity Classical Academy. October 19, 2015. https://www.youtube.com/watch?v=vl802lHAk5Y.

Nelson, Richard William. *Darwin, Then and Now.* Bloomington, IN; iUniverse, 2009.

"Nucleic Acids – DNA and RNA Structure." MEDSimplified. November 16, 2017. https://www.youtube.com/watch?v=0lZRAShqft0.

Seegert, Jay. *Creation & Evolution*. Green Forest, AR: Master Books, 2014.

Strobel, Lee. *The Case for Christ*. Grand Rapids, MI: Zondervan, 1998.

Wallace, J. Warner. *Cold-Case Christianity*. Colorado Springs, CO: David C. Cook, 2013.

"What Is the Evidence for Evolution?" BioLogos. Accessed March 5, 2022, https://biologos.org/common-questions/what-is-the-evidence-for-evolution.

ENDNOTE

Chapter 10

1. Charles Darwin, *The Origin of Species by Means of Natural Selection* (London: John Murray, 1876), 143–144.
2. Samuel Bowring, quoted in J. Madeleine Nash, "When Life Exploded," *Time* 146 (December 4, 1995).
3. Lad Allen, W. Peter Allen, Jonathan Witt, et al., *The Privileged Planet: The Search for Purpose in the Universe* (2004; Murieta, CA: Illustra Media), DVD.

Chapter 26

1. Yuval Noah Harari, *Homo Deus: A Brief History of Tomorrow* (New York: HarperCollins Publishers, 2015), 126.